The Best Christmas Stories Ever

The Best Christmas Stories Ever

AN
APPLE
PAPERBACK

SCHOLASTIC INC.
New York Toronto London Auckland Sydney

ISBN 0-590-45168-5

Copyright © 1991 by Scholastic Inc. All rights reserved. Published by Scholastic Inc. *The Birds' Christmas Carol* was previously published by Scholastic Inc. in 1972. APPLE PAPERBACKS is a registered trademark of Scholastic Inc.

12 11 10 9 8 7 6 5 4 3 2 1   1 2 3 4 5 6/9

Printed in the U.S.A.   40

First Scholastic printing, October 1991

Contents

The Gift of the Magi

O. Henry

ONE DOLLAR AND EIGHTY-SEVEN CENTS. THAT WAS ALL. And sixty cents of it was in pennies. Pennies saved one and two at a time by bulldozing the grocer and the vegetable man and the butcher until one's cheeks burned with the silent imputation of parsimony that such close dealing implied. Three times Della counted it. One dollar and eight-seven cents. And the next day would be Christmas.

There was clearly nothing to do but flop down on the shabby little couch and howl. So Della did it. Which instigates the moral reflection that life is made up of sobs, sniffles, and smiles, with sniffles predominating.

While the mistress of the home is gradually subsiding from the first stage to the second, take a look at the home. A furnished flat at eight dollars per week. It did not exactly beggar description, but it certainly had that word on the lookout for the mendicancy squad.

In the vestibule below was a letter-box into which no letter would go, and an electric button from which no mortal finger could coax a ring. Also appertaining thereunto was a card bearing the name "Mr. James Dillingham Young."

The "Dillingham" had been flung to the breeze during a former period of prosperity when its possessor was being paid thirty dollars per week. Now, when the income was shrunk to twenty dollars, the letters of "Dillingham" looked blurred, as though they were thinking seriously of contracting to a modest and unassuming D. But whenever Mr. James Dillingham Young came home and reached his flat above he was called "Jim" and greatly hugged by Mrs. James Dillingham Young, already introduced to you as Della. Which is all very good.

Della finished her cry and attended to her cheeks with a powder puff. She stood by the window and looked out dully at a gray cat walking a gray fence in a gray back yard. Tomorrow would be Christmas Day, and she had only $1.87 with which to buy Jim a present. She had been saving every penny she could for months, with this result. Twenty dollars a week doesn't go far. Expenses had been greater than she had calculated. They always are. Only $1.87 to buy a present for Jim. Her Jim. Many a happy hour she had spent planning for something nice for him. Something fine and rare and sterling — something just a little bit near to being worthy of the honor of being owned by Jim.

There was a pier-glass between the windows of the room. Perhaps you have seen a pier-glass in an eight-dollar flat. A very thin and very agile person may, by observing his reflection in a rapid sequence of longitudinal strips, obtain a fairly accurate conception of his looks. Della, being slender, had mastered the art.

Suddenly she whirled from the window and stood before the glass. Her eyes were shining brilliantly, but her face had lost its color within twenty seconds. Rapidly she pulled down her hair and let it fall to its full length.

Now, there were two possessions of the James Dillingham Youngs in which they both took a mighty pride. One was Jim's gold watch that had been his father's and his grandfather's. The other was Della's hair. Had the Queen of Sheba lived in the flat across the airshaft, Della would have let her hair hang out the window some day to dry just to depreciate Her Majesty's jewels and gifts. Had King Solomon been the janitor, with all his treasures piled up in the basement, Jim would have pulled out his watch every day he passed, just to see him pluck at his beard from envy.

So now Della's beautiful hair fell about her, rippling and shining like a cascade of brown waters. She did it up again nervously and quickly. Once she faltered for a minute and stood still while a tear or two splashed on the worn red carpet.

On went her old brown jacket, on went her old brown hat. With a whirl of skirts and with the brilliant sparkle still in her eyes, she fluttered out the door and down the stairs to the street.

Where she stopped the sign read: "Mme. Sofronie. Hair Goods of All Kinds." One flight up Della ran, and collected herself, panting. Madame, large, too white, chilly, hardly looked the "Sofronie."

"Will you buy my hair?" asked Della.

"I buy hair," said Madame. "Take yer hat off and let's have a sight at the looks of it."

Down rippled the brown cascade.

"Twenty dollars," said Madame, lifting the mass with a practiced hand.

"Give it to me quick," said Della.

Oh, and the next two hours tripped by on rosy wings. Forget the hashed metaphor. She was ransacking the stores for Jim's present.

She found it at last. It surely had been made for Jim and no one else. There was no other like it in any of the stores, and she had turned all of them inside out. It was a platinum watch-chain, simple and chaste in design, properly proclaiming its value by substance alone and not by meretricious ornamentation — as all good things should do. It was even worthy of The Watch. As soon as she saw it she knew that it must be Jim's. It was like him. Quietness and value — the description applied to both. Twenty-one dollars they took from her for it, and she hurried home with the eighty-seven cents. With that chain on his watch Jim might be properly anxious about the time in any company. Grand as the watch was, he sometimes looked at it on the sly on account of the old leather strap that he used in place of a chain.

When Della reached home her intoxication gave way a little to prudence and reason. She got out her curling-irons and lighted the gas and went to work repairing the ravages made by generosity added to love. Which is always a tremendous task, dear friends — a mammoth task.

Within forty minutes her head was covered with tiny close-lying curls that made her look wonderfully like a truant schoolboy. She looked at her reflection in the mirror long, carefully, and critically.

"If Jim doesn't kill me," she said to herself, "before he takes a second look at me, he'll say I look like a Coney Island chorus girl. But what could I do — Oh! what could I do with a dollar and eighty-seven cents?"

At seven o'clock the coffee was made and the frying-pan was on the back of the stove, hot and ready to cook the chops.

Jim was never late. Della doubled the watch-chain in her hand and sat on the corner of the table near the door that he always entered. Then she heard his step in the stair way down on the first flight, and she turned white for just a moment. She had a habit of saying little silent prayers about the simplest everyday things, and now she whispered, "Please

God, make him think I am still pretty."

The door opened and Jim stepped in and closed it. He looked thin and very serious. Poor fellow, he was only twenty-two — and to be burdened with a family! He needed a new overcoat and he was without gloves.

Jim stepped inside the door, as immovable as a setter at the scent of quail. His eyes were fixed upon Della, and there was an expression in them that she could not read, and it terrified her. It was not anger, nor surprise, nor disapproval, nor horror, nor any of the sentiments that she had been prepared for. He simply stared at her fixedly with that peculiar expression on his face.

Della wriggled off the table and went for him.

"Jim, darling," she cried, "don't look at me that way. I had my hair cut off and sold it because I couldn't have lived through Christmas without giving you a present. It'll grow out again — you won't mind, will you? I just had to do it. My hair grows awfully fast. Say 'Merry Christmas!' Jim, and let's be happy. You don't know what a nice — what a beautiful, nice gift I've got for you."

"You've cut off your hair?" asked Jim, laboriously, as if he had not arrived at that patent fact yet even after the hardest mental labor.

"Cut it off and sold it," said Della. "Don't you like me just as well, anyhow? I'm me without my hair, ain't I?'"

Jim looked about the room curiously.

"You say your hair is gone?" he said, with an air almost of idiocy.

"You needn't look for it," said Della. "It's sold, I tell you — sold and gone, too. It's Christmas Eve, boy. Be good to me, for it went for you. Maybe the hairs of my head were numbered," she went on with a sudden serious sweetness, "but nobody could ever count my love for you. Shall I put the chops on, Jim?"

Out of his trance Jim seemed to quickly wake. He enfolded his Della. For ten seconds let us regard with discreet scrutiny some inconsequential object in the other direction. Eight dollars a week or a million a year — what is the difference? A mathematician or a wit would give you the wrong answer. The Magi brought valuable gifts, but that was not among them. This dark assertion will be illuminated later on.

Jim drew a package from his overcoat pocket and threw it upon the table.

"Don't make any mistake, Dell," he said, "about me. I don't think there's anything in the way of a haircut or a shave or a shampoo that could make me like my girl any less. But if you'll unwrap that package you may see why you had me going awhile at first."

White fingers and nimble tore at the string and paper. And then an ecstatic scream of joy; and then, alas! a quick feminine change to hysterical tears and wails, necessitating the immediate employment of all the comforting powers of the lord of the flat.

For there lay The Combs — the set of combs that Della had worshiped for long in a Broadway window. Beautiful combs, pure tortoise shell, with jeweled rims — just the shade to wear in the beautiful vanished hair. They were expensive combs, she knew, and her heart had simply craved and yearned over them without the least hope of possession. And now they were hers, but the tresses that should have adorned the coveted adornments were gone.

But she hugged them to her bosom, and at length she was able to look up with dim eyes and a smile and say: "My hair grows so fast, Jim!"

And then Della leaped up like a little singed cat and cried, "Oh, oh!"

Jim had not yet seen his beautiful present. She held it out to him eagerly upon her open palm. The dull precious metal seemed to flash with a reflection of her bright and ardent spirit.

"Isn't it a dandy, Jim? I hunted all over town to find it. You'll have to look at the time a hundred times a day now. Give me your watch. I want to see how it looks on it."

Instead of obeying, Jim tumbled down on the couch and put his hands under the back of his head and smiled.

"Dell," he said, "let's put our Christmas presents away and keep 'em awhile. They're too nice to use just at present. I sold the watch to get the money to buy your combs. And now suppose you put the chops on."

The Magi, as you know, were wise men — wonderfully wise men — who brought gifts to the Babe in the manger. They invented the art of giving Christmas presents. Being wise, their gifts were no doubt wise ones, possibly bearing the privilege of exchange in case of duplication. And here I have lamely related to you the uneventful chronicle of two foolish children in a flat who most unwisely sacrificed for each other the greatest treasures of their house. But in a last word to the wise of these days let it be said that of all who give gifts these two were the wisest. Of all who give and receive gifts, such as they are wisest. Everywhere they are wisest. They are the Magi.

The Fir-Tree

Hans Christian Andersen

OUT IN THE WOODS STOOD A NICE LITTLE FIR-TREE. THE place he had was a very good one; the sun shone on him; as to fresh air, there was enough of that, and round him grew many large-sized comrades, pines as well as firs. But the little Fir wanted so very much to be a grown-up tree.

He did not think of the warm sun and of the fresh air; he did not care for the little cottage-children that ran about and prattled when they were in the woods looking for wild strawberries. The children often came with a whole pitcher full of berries, or a long row of them threaded on a straw, and sat down near the young Tree and said, "O, how pretty he is! What a nice little fir!" But this was what the Tree could not bear to hear.

At the end of a year he had shot up a good deal, and after another year, he was another long bit taller; for with fir-trees one can always tell by the shoots how many years old they are.

"O, were I but such a high tree as the others are," sighed he. "Then I should be able to spread out my branches, and with the tops to look into the wide world! Then would the birds build nests among my branches; and when there was a breeze, I could bend with as much stateliness as the others!"

Neither the sunbeams, nor the birds, nor the red clouds which morning and evening sailed above him, gave the little Tree any pleasure.

In winter, when the snow lay glittering on the ground, a hare would often come leaping along, and jump right over the little Tree. O, that made him so angry! But two winters were past, and in the third the Tree was so large that the hare was obliged to go round it. "To grow and grow, to get older and be tall," thought the Tree; "that, after all, is the most delightful thing in the world!"

In autumn the wood-cutters always came and felled some of the largest trees. This happened every year; and the young Fir-tree, that had now grown to a very comely size, trembled at the sight; for the magnificent great trees fell to the earth with noise and crackling, the branches were lopped off, and the trees looked long and bare: they were hardly to be recognized; and then they were laid in carts, and the horses dragged them out of the wood.

Where did they go to? What became of them?

In spring, when the Swallows and the Storks came, the Tree asked them, "Don't you know where they have been taken? Have you not met them anywhere?"

The Swallows did not know anything about it; but the Stork looked musing, nodded his head, and said, "Yes; I think I know; I met many ships as I was flying hither from Egypt; on the ships were magnificent masts, and I venture to assert that it was they that smelt so of fir. I may congratulate you, for they lifted themselves on high most majestically!"

"O, were I but old enough to fly across the sea! But how does the sea look in reality? What is it like?"

"That would take a long time to explain," said the Stork, and with these words off he went.

"Rejoice in thy growth!" said the Sunbeams; "rejoice in thy vigorous growth, and in the fresh life that moveth within thee!"

And the Wind kissed the Tree, and the Dew wept tears over him; but the Fir understood it not.

When Christmas came, quite young trees were cut

down; trees which often were not even as large or of the same age as this Fir-tree, who could never rest, but always wanted to be off. These young trees, and they were always the finest looking, retained their branches; they were laid on carts, and the horses drew them out of the wood.

"Where are they going to?" asked the Fir. "They are no taller than I —" there was one indeed that was considerably shorter — "and why do they retain all their branches? Whither are they taken?"

"We know! we know!" chirped the Sparrows. "We have peeped in at the windows in the town below! We know whither they are taken! The greatest splendor and the greatest magnificence one can imagine await them. We peeped through the windows, and saw them planted in the middle of the warm room, and ornamented with the most splendid things — with gilded apples, with gingerbread, with toys, and many hundred lights!"

"And then?" asked the Fir-tree, trembling in every bough. "And then? What happens then?"

"We did not see anything more: it was incomparably beautiful."

"I would fain know if I am destined for so glorious a career," cried the Tree, rejoicing. "That is still better than to cross the sea! What a longing do I suffer! Were Christmas but come! I am now tall, and my branches spread like the others that were carried off last year! O, were I but already on the cart! Were I in the warm room with all the splendor and magnificence! Yes; then something better, something still grander, will surely follow, or wherefore should they thus ornament me? Something better, something still grander, *must* follow — but what?

O, how I long, how I suffer! I do not know myself what is the matter with me!"

"Rejoice in our presence!" said the Air and the Sunlight; "rejoice in thy own fresh youth!"

But the Tree did not rejoice at all; he grew and grew, and was green both winter and summer. People that saw him said, "What a fine tree!" and towards Christmas he was one of the first that was cut down. The axe stuck deep into the very pith; the Tree fell to the earth with a sigh: he felt a pang — it was like a swoon; he could not think of happiness, for he was sorrowful at being separated from his home, from the place where he had sprung up. He well knew that he should never see his dear old comrades, the little bushes and flowers around him, any more; perhaps not even the birds! The departure was not at all agreeable.

The Tree only came to himself when he was unloaded in a court-yard with the other trees, and heard a man say, "That one is splendid! we don't want the others." Then two servants came in rich livery and carried the Fir-tree into a large and splendid drawing-room. Portraits were hanging on the walls, and near the white porcelain stove stood two large Chinese vases with lions on the covers. There, too, were large easy-chairs, silken sofas, large tables full of picture-books, and full of toys worth hundreds and hundreds of crowns — at least the children said so. And the Fir-tree was stuck upright in a cask that was filled with sand: but no one could see that it was a cask, for green cloth was hung all round it, and it stood on a large gayly-colored carpet. O, how the tree quivered! What was to happen? The servants, as well as the young ladies, decorated it. On one branch there were hung little nets cut out of colored paper, and each net was filled with sugar-plums; and among the other boughs gilded apples and walnuts were suspended, looking as though they had grown there, and little blue and white tapers were placed among the leaves. Dolls that looked for all the world like men — the Tree had never beheld such before — were seen among the foliage, and at the very top a large star of gold tinsel was fixed. It was really splendid — beyond description splendid.

"This evening!" said they all; "how it will shine this evening!"

"O," thought the Tree, "if the evening were but come! If the tapers were but lighted! And then I wonder what will happen! Perhaps the other trees from the forest will come to look at me! Perhaps the sparrows will beat against the window-panes! I wonder if I shall take root here, and winter and summer stand covered with ornaments!"

He knew very much about the matter! But he was so impatient that for sheer longing he got a pain in his back, and this with trees is the same thing as a headache with us.

The candles were now lighted. What brightness! What splendor! The Tree trembled so in every bough that one of the tapers set fire to the foilage. It blazed up splendidly.

"Help! help!" cried the young ladies, and they quickly put out the fire.

Now the Tree did not even dare tremble. What a state he was in! He was so uneasy lest he should lose something of his splendor, that he was quite bewildered amidst the glare and brightness; when suddenly both folding-doors opened, and a troop of children rushed in as if they would upset the Tree. The older persons followed quietly; the little ones stood quite still. But it was only for a moment; then they shouted so that the whole place re-echoed with their rejoicing; they danced round the Tree, and one present after the other was pulled off.

"What are they about?" thought the Tree. "What is to happen now!" And the lights burned down to the very branches, and as they burned down they were put out one after the other, and then the children had permission to plunder the Tree. So they fell upon it with such violence that all its branches cracked; if it had not been fixed firmly in the cask, it would certainly have tumbled down.

The children danced about with their beautiful playthings: no one looked at the Tree except the old nurse, who peeped between the branches; but it was only to see if there was a fig or an apple left that had been forgotten.

"A story! a story!" cried the children, drawing a little fat man towards the Tree. He seated himself under it, and said, "Now we are in the shade, and the Tree can listen too. But I shall tell only one story. Now which will you have; about Ivedy-Avedy, or about Klumpy-Dumpy who tumbled downstairs, and yet after all came to the throne and married the princess?"

"Ivedy-Avedy," cried some; "Klumpy-Dumpy," cried the others. There was such a bawling and screaming! — the Fir-tree alone was silent, and he thought to himself, "Am I not to bawl with the rest? — am I to do nothing whatever?" for he was one of the company, and had done what he had to do.

And the man told about Klumpy-Dumpy that tumbled down, who notwithstanding came to the throne, and at last married the princess. And the children clapped their hands, and cried out, "O, go on! Do go on!" They wanted to hear about Ivedy-Avedy too, but the little man only told them about Klumpy-Dumpy. The Fir-tree stood quite still and absorbed in thought: the birds in the wood had never related the like of this. "Klumpy-Dumpy fell downstairs, and yet he married the princess! Yes, yes! that's the way of the world!" thought the Fir-tree, and believed it all, because the man who told the story was so good-looking. "Well, well! who knows, perhaps I may fall downstairs too, and get a princess as wife!" And he looked forward with joy to the morrow, when he hoped to be decked out again with lights, playthings, fruits, and tinsel.

"I won't tremble to-morrow!" thought the Fir-tree. "I will enjoy to the full all my splendor! To-morrow I shall hear again the story of Klumpy-Dumpy, and perhaps that of Ivedy-Avedy too." And the whole night the Tree stood still in deep thought.

In the morning the servant and the housemaid came in.

"Now then the splendor will begin again," thought the Fir. But they dragged him out of the room, and up the stairs into the loft; and here in a dark corner, where no daylight could enter, they left him. "What's the meaning of this?" thought the Tree. "What am I to do here? What shall I hear now, I wonder?" And he leaned against the wall lost in reverie. Time enough had he too for his reflections; for days and nights passed on, and nobody came up; and when at last somebody did come, it was only to put some great trunks in a corner out of the way. There stood the Tree quite hidden; it seemed as if he had been entirely forgotten.

" 'Tis now winter out-of-doors!" thought the Tree. "The earth is hard and covered with snow; men cannot plant me now, and therefore I have been put up here under shelter till the spring-time comes! How thoughtful that is! How kind man is, after all! If it only were not so dark here, and so terribly lonely! Not even a hare. And out in the woods it was so pleasant, when the snow was on the ground and the hare leaped by; yes — even when he jumped over me; but I did not like it then. It is really terribly lonely here!"

"Squeak! squeak!" said a little Mouse at the same moment, peeping out of his hole. And then another little one came. They snuffed about the Fir-tree, and rustled among the branches.

"It is dreadfully cold," said the Mouse. "But for that, it would be delightful here, old Fir, wouldn't it?"

"I am by no means old," said the Fir-tree. "There's many a one considerably older than I am."

"Where do you come from," asked the Mice; "and what can you do?" They were so extremely curious. "Tell us about the most beautiful spot on the earth. Have you never been there? Were you never in the larder, where cheeses lie on the shelves, and hams hang from above; where one dances about on tallow candles; that place where one enters lean, and comes out again fat and portly?"

"I know no such place," said the Tree. "But I know the wood, where the sun shines, and where the little birds sing." And then he told all about his youth; and the little Mice had never heard the like before, and they listened and said,

"Well, to be sure! How much you have seen! How happy you must have been!"

"I!" said the Fir-tree, thinking over what he had himself related. "Yes, in reality those were happy times." And then he told about Christmas Eve, when he was decked out with cakes and candles.

"O," said the little Mice, "how fortunate you have been, old Fir-tree!"

"I am by no means old," said he. "I came from the wood this winter; I am in my prime, and am only rather short for my age."

"What delightful stories you know!" said the Mice: and the next night they came with four other little Mice, who were to hear what the Tree recounted; and the more he related, the more plainly he remembered all himself; and it appeared as if those times had really been happy times. "But they may still come — they may still come. Klumpy-Dumpy fell downstairs, and yet he got a princess!" and he thought at the moment of a nice little Birch-tree growing out in the woods: to the Fir, that would be a real charming princess.

"Who is Klumpy-Dumpy?" asked the Mice. So then the Fir-tree told the whole fairy tale, for he could remember every single word of it; and the little Mice jumped for joy up to the very top of the Tree. Next night two more Mice came, and on Sunday two Rats, even; but they said the stories were not interesting, which vexed the little Mice; and they, too, now began to think them not so very amusing either.

"Do you know only one story?" asked the Rats.

"Only that one," answered the Tree. "I heard it on my happiest evening, but I did not then know how happy I was."

"It is a very stupid story! Don't you know one about bacon and tallow candles? Can't you tell any larder-stories?"

"No," said the Tree.

"Then good-by," said the Rats; and they went home.

At last the little Mice stayed away also; and the Tree sighed: "After all, it was very pleasant when the sleek little Mice sat round me and listened to what I told them. Now that too is over. But I will take good care to enjoy myself when I am brought out again."

But when was that to be? Why, one morning there came a quantity of people and set to work in the loft. The trunks were moved, the tree was pulled out and thrown — rather hard, it is true — down on the floor, but a man drew him towards the stairs, where the day-light shone.

"Now a merry life will begin again," thought the Tree. He felt the fresh air, the first sunbeam, and now he was out in the court-yard. All passed so quickly, there was so much going on around him, that the Tree quite forgot to look to himself. The court adjoined a garden, and all was in flower; the roses hung so fresh and odorous over the balustrade, the lindens were in blossom, the Swallows flew by, and said, "Quirre-vit! my husband is come!" but it was not the Fir-tree that they meant.

22

"Now, then, I shall really enjoy life," said he, exultingly, and spread out his branches; but, alas! they were all withered and yellow. It was in a corner that he lay, among weeds and nettles. The golden star of tinsel was still on the top of the Tree, and glittered in the sunshine.

In the court-yard some of the merry children were playing who had danced at Christmas round the Fir-tree, and were so glad at the sight of him. One of the youngest ran and tore off the golden star.

"Only look what is still on the ugly old Christmas tree!" said he, trampling on the branches, so that they all cracked beneath his feet.

And the Tree beheld all the beauty of the flowers, and the freshness in the garden; he beheld himself, and wished he had remained in his dark corner in the loft: he thought of his first youth in the wood, of the merry Christmas Eve, and of the little Mice, who had listened with so much pleasure to the story of Klumpy-Dumpy.

" 'Tis over — 'tis past!" said the poor Tree. "Had I but rejoiced when I had reason to do so! But now 'tis past, 'tis past!"

And the gardener's boy chopped the Tree into small pieces; there was a whole heap lying there. The wood flamed up splendidly under the large brewing copper, and it sighed so deeply! Each sigh was like a shot.

The boys played about in the court, and the youngest wore the gold star on his breast, which the Tree had had on the happiest evening of his life. However, that was over now — the Tree gone, the story at an end. All, all was over; every tale must end at last.

The Birds' Christmas Carol

Kate Douglas Wiggin

1.
A Little Snow Bird

It was very early Christmas morning, and in the stillness of the dawn, with the soft snow falling on the housetops, a little child was born in the Bird household.

They had intended to name the baby Lucy, if it was a girl; but they had not expected her on Christmas morning, and a name for a real Christmas baby must be something special — the whole family agreed on that.

Mr. Bird said that he had assisted in naming the three boys — Donald, Paul, and Hugh — and that he should leave the naming of the girl entirely to Mrs. Bird. Donald Junior wanted his sister called "Dorothy," and Paul chose "Luella." But Uncle Jack said that the first girl should always be named for her mother, no matter how hideous the name happened to be.

Grandma said that she would prefer not to take any part in the discussion, and then everybody suddenly remembered that Mrs. Bird had thought of naming the baby Lucy, for Grandma herself — so naturally no one expected Grandma to suggest another name.

Hugh, who until then had been "the baby," sat in one corner and said nothing. There was a newer baby now, and the "first girl," too, — and it made him actually green with jealousy.

But it was too important a matter to be settled until Mamma had been consulted.

Meanwhile Mrs. Bird lay in her room, sleepy and happy with her sweet girl baby by her side. Nurse was downstairs in the kitchen, and the room was dim and quiet. There was a cheerful open fire in the grate; but though the shutters were closed, the side windows that looked out on the church next door were a little open.

Suddenly a sound of music poured out into the bright air and drifted into the chamber. It was the boy-choir singing Christmas anthems. Higher and higher rose the clear, fresh voices, full of hope and cheer, as children's voices always are. Fuller and fuller grew the burst of melody as one glad strain fell upon another in joyful harmony:

> "Carol, brothers, carol,
>   Carol joyfully,
> Carol the good tidings,
>   Carol merrily!
> And pray a gladsome Christmas
>   For all your fellow men:
> Carol, brothers, carol,
>   Christmas Day again."

One verse followed another, always with the same glad refrain:

"And pray a gladsome Christmas
    For all your fellow men:
Carol, brothers, carol,
    Christmas Day again."

Mrs. Bird thought, as the music floated in upon her gentle sleep, that she had slipped into heaven with her new baby, and that the angels were bidding them welcome. But the tiny bundle by her side stirred a little, and though it was scarcely more than the ruffling of a feather, she awoke.

She opened her eyes and drew the baby closer. She looked like a rose dipped in milk, Mrs. Bird thought, like a pink cherub, with its halo of pale yellow hair, finer than floss silk.

"Carol, brothers, carol
    Carol, joyfully,
Carol the good tidings,
    Carol merrily!"

The voices were brimming over with joy.

"Why, my baby," whispered Mrs. Bird in soft surprise, "I had forgotten what day it was. You are a little Christmas child, and we will name you 'Carol' — mother's little Christmas Carol!"

"What!" said Mr. Bird, coming in softly.

"Why, Donald, don't you think 'Carol' is a sweet name for a Christmas baby? It came to me just a moment ago in the singing, as I was lying here half asleep and half awake."

"I think it is a charming name, dear heart. It sounds just like you, and I hope that, being a girl, this baby has some chance of being as lovely as her mother." At this speech from the baby's papa, Mrs. Bird blushed with happiness.

And so Carol came by her name.

Uncle Jack declared laughingly that it was very strange if a whole family of Birds could not be indulged in a single Carol; and Grandma, who adored the child, thought the name much more appropriate than Lucy.

Perhaps because she was born in holiday time, Carol was a very happy baby. Of course, she was too tiny to understand the joy of Christmas-tide, but people say there is everything in a good beginning; and she may have breathed in unconsciously the fragrance of evergreens and holiday dinners, while the peals of sleigh bells and the laughter of happy children may have fallen upon her baby ears and wakened in them a glad surprise at the merry world she had come to live in.

Her cheeks and lips were as red as holly berries; her hair was for all the world the color of a Christmas candle flame; her eyes were bright as stars; her laugh like a chime of Christmas bells; and her tiny hands forever outstretched in giving.

Such a generous little creature! A spoonful of bread and milk always had to be taken by Mamma or Nurse before Carol could enjoy her supper; whatever bit of cake or sweet found its way into her pretty fingers was straightway broken in half to be shared with Donald, Paul, or Hugh; and when they made believe nibble the morsel, she would clap her hands and crow with delight.

"Why does she do it?" asked Donald, thoughtfully. "None of us boys ever did."

"I hardly know," said Mamma, catching her darling to her heart. "Perhaps because she is a little Christmas child."

2.
Drooping Wings

IT WAS DECEMBER, TEN YEARS LATER.

Carol had seen nine Christmas trees lighted on her birthdays, one after another; nine times she had helped in the holiday festivities of the household, and for five years, certainly, she had hidden presents for Mamma and Papa in their own bureau drawers.

For five years she had heard "Twas the night before Christmas," and hung up a scarlet stocking many sizes too large for her, and pinned a sprig of holly on her little white nightgown, to show Santa Claus that she was "truly" a Christmas child, and dreamed of fur-coated saints and toy-packs and reindeer, and wished everybody a "Merry Christmas" before it was light in the morning, and lent every one of her new toys to the neighbors' children before noon, and eaten turkey and plum pudding, and gone to bed at night in a trance of happiness at the day's pleasures.

Donald was away at college now. Paul and Hugh were great manly fellows, taller than their mother. Papa Bird had gray hairs in his whiskers; and Grandma, God bless her, had been four Chrismases in heaven.

But there was another reason why Christmas in the Birds' Nest was not as merry now as it used to be. The little child that had once brought such an added joy to Christmas Day, now lay, month after month, a patient, helpless invalid, in the room where she was born.

Carol had never been very strong in body, and it was with a pang of terror that her mother and father noticed her beginning to limp slightly, soon after she was five years old. She also complained often of weariness and would nestle close to her mother saying she "would rather not go out to play, please."

The illness was slight at first, and hope was always stirring in Mrs. Bird's heart. "Carol will feel stronger in the summertime," she would say. Or "Carol will be better when she has spent a year in the country"; or "She will outgrow it"; or "We will try a new physician."

But slowly it became plain even to Mrs. Bird that no physician on earth could make Carol strong again; and that no "summertime" nor "country air," unless it was the everlasting summertime in a heavenly country, could bring the little girl back to health.

The cheeks and lips that were once as red as holly berries faded to faint pink; the starlike eyes grew softer, for they often gleamed through tears; and the gay child-laugh, that had been like a chime of Christmas bells, gave place to a smile so lovely, so touching, so tender and patient, that it filled the very house with a gentle radiance.

The love they all felt for her could do nothing. And when we have said that we have said all, for love is stronger than anything else in the world. Mr. and Mrs. Bird were talking it over one evening when all the children were asleep. A famous physician had visited them that day, and told them that some time, it might be in one year, it might be in more, Carol would slip quietly off forever.

"It is no use for us to shut our eyes to it any longer," said Mr. Bird, as he paced up and down the library floor. "Carol will never be well again. It seems as if I could not bear it when I think of that loveliest child doomed to lie there day after day, and, what is more, to suffer pain that we are helpless to keep away from her. Merry Christmas, indeed! It gets to be the saddest day in the year to me!"

And poor Mr. Bird sank into a chair by the table, and buried his face in his hands to keep his wife from seeing the tears that would come in spite of all his efforts.

"But, Donald, dear," said Mrs. Bird, in a trembling voice, "Christmas Day may not be so merry with us as it used to be, but it is a happy and blessed day even so, and that is almost better. I suffer for Carol's sake, but I have almost given up being sorrowful for my own. I am too happy in the child, and I see so clearly what she has done for us and the other children. Donald and Paul and Hugh were three strong, willful, boisterous boys. But now you seldom see such tenderness, devotion, thought for others, and self-denial in boys of their years. A quarrel or a hot word is almost unknown in this house. Why? Because Carol would hear it and it would distress her, she is so full of love and goodness. What's more, the boys study as hard as they can. Why? Partly, at least, because they like to teach Carol, and amuse her by telling her what they read. Everyone loves to be in Carol's room, because there they can forget their own troubles. And as for me, Donald, I am a better woman every day for Carol's sake. I have to be her strength, her hope; and she, my own little child, is my example!"

"I was wrong, dear heart," said Mr. Bird more cheerfully. "We will try not to sorrow, but to rejoice instead, that we have an 'angel of the house' like Carol."

"And as for her future," Mrs. Bird went on, "I think we need not be overanxious. I feel as if she did not belong altogether to us, but that when she has done what God sent her for, He will take her back to Himself — and it may not be very long!" Here it was poor Mrs. Bird's turn to break down, and Mr. Bird's turn to comfort her.

3.
Bird's Nest

CAROL HERSELF KNEW NOTHING OF HER MOTHER'S TEARS nor her father's anxieties. They hid their feelings, knowing their sadness would distress her. So she lived on peacefully in the room where she was born.

But you never would have known that room. You see, Mr. Bird had a great deal of money. And though he felt sometimes as if he wanted to throw it all in the ocean, since it could not buy a strong body for his little girl, still he was glad that he could use his money to make the place Carol lived in just as beautiful as it could be.

The room had been extended by building a large addition that hung out over the garden below. It was a kind of sun porch, and it was so filled with windows and plants that it might have been a greenhouse. The ones on the side were even nearer the little church next door than they used to be. Those in front looked out on the beautiful harbor. And although those in the back commanded a view of nothing more than a little alley, nevertheless they were pleasantest of all, for the Ruggles family lived in a house in that alley, and the nine Ruggles children were a source of endless interest to Carol.

The window shutters could all be opened and Carol could take a real sun bath in this lovely glass house, or they could all be closed when her head ached or her eyes were tired. The carpet was a soft gray, with clusters of green bay and holly leaves. The furniture was painted white, and on each piece an artist had painted snow scenes and ringing bells and singing carols.

Donald had made a polished shelf and screwed it on the outside of the footboard of the bed, and the boys always kept this full of blooming plants, which they changed from time to time. The headboard, too, had a bracket on either side, where there were pots of maidenhair ferns.

In the windows were golden cages in which lovebirds and canaries sang. They, poor caged things, could hop as far from their wooden perches as Carol could venture from her little white bed.

On one side of the room was a bookcase filled with hundreds — yes, I mean it — with hundreds of books; books with gay-colored pictures, books without; books with black and white sketches, books with none at all; books with verses, books with stories; books that made children laugh, and some that made them cry; books with words of one syllable for tiny boys and girls, and books with words of fearful length to puzzle wise ones.

This was Carol's "circulating library." Every Saturday she chose ten books, jotting their names down in a little diary. Into these books she slipped cards that said: "Please keep this book two weeks and read it. With love, Carol Bird."

Then Mrs. Bird stepped into her carriage and took the ten books to the Children's Hospital, and brought home ten others that she had left there the fortnight before.

These books were a source of great happiness; for some of the Hospital children that were old enough to print or write, and were strong enough to do it, wrote Carol sweet little letters about the books, and she answered them, and they grew to be friends. (You do not always have to see people to love them.)

There was a shoulder-high wood ledge about the room, and on top of this, in a narrow gilt framework, ran a row of illuminated pictures, illustrating fairy tales, all in dull blue and gold and scarlet and silver. From the door to the closet there was the story of "The Fair One with Golden Locks"; from closet to bookcase, ran "Puss in Boots"; from bookcase to fireplace, was "Jack the Giant-Killer"; and on the other side of the room were "Hop o' My Thumb," "The Sleeping Beauty," and "Cinderella."

Then there was a great closet full of beautiful things to wear, but they were all dressing gowns and slippers and shawls; and there were drawers full of toys and games, but they were such as you could play with on your lap. There were no skates nor balls, nor bean bags, nor tennis rackets; but, after all, other children needed these more than Carol Bird, for she was always happy and contented, whatever she had or whatever she lacked; and on her eighth Christmas after the room had been made so lovely for her, she called herself, in fun, a "bird of paradise."

On these particular December days she was happier than usual, for Uncle Jack was coming from Europe to spend the holidays. Dear, funny, jolly, loving, wise Uncle

Jack, who came every two or three years, and brought so much joy with him that the world looked as black as a thundercloud for a week after he went away again.

The mail had brought this letter:

London, Nov. 28th, 188 —

Wish you merry Christmas, you dearest birdlings in America! Preen your feathers, and stretch the Birds' Nest a little, if you please, and let Uncle Jack in for the holidays. I am coming with such a trunk full of treasures that you'll have to borrow the stockings of a giant and giantess; I am coming to squeeze a certain little lady bird until she cries for mercy; I am coming to see if I can find a boy to take care of a little black pony that I bought lately. It's the strangest thing I ever knew; I've hunted all over Europe, and can't find a boy to suit me! I'll tell you why. I've set my heart on finding one with a dimple in his chin, because this pony particularly likes dimples! ["Hurrah!" cried Hugh. "I'll never be ashamed of my dimple again."]

Please drop a note to the clerk of the weather, and have a good, rousing snowstorm — say on the twenty-second. None of your meek, gentle nonsensical, shilly-shallying snowstorms; not the sort where the flakes float lazily down from the sky as if they didn't care whether they ever got here or not and then melt away as soon as they touch the earth, but a regular, businesslike, whizzing, whirring, blurring, cutting snowstorm, warranted to freeze and stay on!

I should like rather a LARGE Christmas tree. We can cut a hole in the roof if the tree chances to be too high for the room.

Tell Bridget to begin to fatten a turkey, and tell her that the pudding must be unusually huge and darkly, deeply, lugubriously blue in color. It must be stuck so full of plums that the pudding itself will ooze out into the pan and not be brought on to the table at all. I expect to be there by the twentieth to manage these things myself, but give you these instructions in case I should be delayed.

And Carol must plead for the snowstorm — the "clerk of the weather" may pay some attention to her as she is a Christmas child. And she must look up the boy with the dimple for me — she's likelier to find him than I am, this minute. She must advise about the turkey, and Bridget must bring the pudding to her bedside and let her drop every separate plum into it and stir it once for luck, or I'll not eat a single slice — for Carol is the dearest part of Christmas to Uncle Jack, and he'll have none of it without her. She is better than all the turkeys and puddings and apples and spareribs and wreaths and garlands and mistletoe and stockings and chimneys and sleigh bells in the world. She is the very sweetest Christmas Carol that was ever written, said, sung, or chanted, and I am coming, as fast as ships and railway trains can carry me, to tell her so.

Carol's joy knew no bounds. Mr. and Mrs. Bird laughed and kissed each other in delight, and when the boys heard it they whooped for joy, until the Ruggles family, whose back yard joined their garden, gathered at the gate and wondered what was up in the big house.

4.
"Birds of a Feather Flock Together"

UNCLE JACK REALLY DID COME ON THE TWENTIETH. He was not detained by business, nor did he get left behind nor snowed up, as frequently happens in stories, and in real life, too. The snowstorm came also; and the turkey. Donald came, too — Donald, with a line of down upon his upper lip, and stores of knowledge in his handsome head, and stories! You couldn't turn over a page without reminding Donald of something that happened "at college." One or the other was always at Carol's bedside, for they fancied her paler than she used to be, and they could not bear her out of sight. It was Uncle Jack, though, who sat beside her in the winter twilights. The room was quiet, and almost dark, save for the snowlight outside and the flickering flame of the fire, that danced over the "Sleeping Beauty's" face and touched the golden locks with ruddier glory. Carol's hand, all too thin and white these days, lay close clasped in Uncle Jack's, and they talked together quietly of many, many things.

"I want to tell you all about my plans for Christmas this year, Uncle Jack," said Carol, on the first evening of his visit, "because it will be the loveliest one I ever had. The boys laugh at me for caring so much about it. But it isn't altogether because it is Chrismas nor because it is my birthday. Long, long ago, when I first began to be ill, I used to think, the first thing when I waked on Christmas morning, 'Today is Christ's birthday — and mine!' And so I do not quite feel about Christmas as other girls do. Mamma says she supposes that ever so many other children have been born on that day. I often wonder where they are, Uncle Jack, and whether it is a dear thought to them, too, or whether I am so much in bed, and so often alone, that it means more to me. Oh, I do hope that none of them are poor, or cold, or hungry; and I wish, I wish they were all as happy as I, because they are really my brothers and sisters. Now, Uncle Jack dear, I am going to try and make somebody happy every single Christmas that I live, and this year it is to be the 'Ruggleses in the rear.'"

"That large and interesting brood of children in the little house at the end of the back garden?"

"Yes. Isn't it nice to see so many together? And, Uncle Jack, why do the big families always seem to live in the little houses, and the little families in the big houses? We ought to call them the Ruggles children, of course; but Donald began talking of them as the 'Ruggleses in the rear,' and Papa and Mamma took it up, and now we cannot seem to help it.

"When they first moved in, I used to sit in my window and watch them play in their back yard; they are so strong, and jolly, and good-natured — and then, one day, I had a terrible headache, and Donald asked them if they would please not scream quite so loud, and they explained that they were having a game of circus, but that they would change and play 'Deaf and Dumb' all the afternoon."

Uncle Jack smiled, "An obliging family, to be sure."

"Yes, we all thought it very kind, and I smiled at them from the window when I was well enough to be up again. Now Sarah Maud comes to her door when the children come home from school, and if Mamma nods her head, 'Yes,' that means 'Carol is very well,' and then you ought to hear the little Ruggleses yell — I believe they try to see how much noise they can make; but if Mamma shakes her head, they always play at quiet games. Then, one day, Cary, my pet canary, flew out of her cage, and Peter Ruggles caught her and brought her back, and he came up here in my room so that I could thank him."

"Is Peter the oldest?"

"No. Sarah Maud is the oldest — she helps do the washing; and Peter is the next. He is a delivery boy."

"And which is the pretty little red-haired girl?"

"That's Kitty."

"And the fat youngster?"

"Baby Larry."

"And that — most — freckled one?"

"Now, don't laugh — that's Peoria."

"Carol, you are joking."

"No, really, Uncle dear. She was born in Peoria; that's all."

"And is the next boy Oshkosh?"

"No," laughed Carol. "The others are Susan, and Clement, and Eily, and Cornelius. They all look pretty much alike except that some have more freckles than the others."

44

"How did you ever learn all their names?"

"Well, I have what I call a 'window school.' It is too cold now, but in warm weather I am wheeled out on my little balcony, and the Ruggleses climb up and walk along our garden fence, and sit down on the roof of our carriage house. That brings them quite near, and I read to them and tell them stories. On Thanksgiving Day they came up for a few minutes — it was quite warm at eleven o'clock — and we told each other what we had to be thankful for. But they gave such queer answers that I couldn't understand them every well. Susan was thankful for trunks of all things in the world; Cornelius, for the horse-car; Kitty, for pork steak; and Clem, who is very quiet, brightened up when I came to him, and said he was thankful for his *lame puppy*. Wasn't that strange?"

"It might teach some of us a lesson, mightn't it, little girl?"

"That's what Mamma said. Now I'm going to give this whole Christmas to the Ruggleses. And, Uncle Jack, I earned part of the money myself."

"You, my bird! How?"

"Well, you see, it could not be my own, own Christmas if Papa gave me all the money, and I decided that I should do something on my very own; and so I talked with Mamma. Of course she thought of something lovely — she always does. Mamma's head is just brimming over with lovely thoughts — all I have to do is ask, and out pops the very one I want. This thought was to let her write down, just as I told her, a description of how a little girl lived in her own room for three years, and what she did to amuse herself. And we sent it to a magazine and got twenty-five dollars for it. Just think!"

"Well, well," cried Uncle Jack, "my little girl is a real author! And what are you going to do with this wonderful 'own' money of yours?"

"I shall give the nine Ruggleses a grand Christmas dinner here in this very room — that will be Papa's contribution — and afterward a beautiful Christmas tree, fairly blooming with presents — that will be my part; for I have another way of adding to my twenty-five dollars so that I can buy everything I like. I should like it very much if you would sit at the head of the table, Uncle Jack, for nobody could ever be frightened of you. Mamma is going to help us, but Papa and the boys are going to eat together downstairs for fear of making the little Ruggleses shy. And after we've had a merry time with the tree and presents, we can open my window and listen to the music at the church if it comes before the children go. I have written a letter to the organist, and asked him if I might have the two songs I like best. Will you see if it is all right?"

Birds' Nest, Dec. 21st, 188–

Dear Mr. Wilkie,

I am the sick girl who lives next door to the church, and, as I seldom go out, the music on practice days and Sundays is one of my greatest pleasures.

I want to know if you can have "Carol, brothers, carol," on Christmas night, and if the boy who sings, "My ain countree" so beautifully may please sing that too. I think it is the loveliest thing in the world, but it always makes me cry; doesn't it you?

46

If it isn't too much trouble, I hope they can sing them both quite early, as after ten o'clock I may be asleep.

Yours respectfully,
CAROL BIRD

P.S. — The reason I like "Carol, brothers, carol," is because the choirboys sang it eleven years ago, the morning I was born, and put it into Mamma's head to call me Carol. She didn't remember then that my other name would be Bird, because she was half asleep, and could only think of one thing at a time. Donald says if I had been born on the Fourth of July they would have named me "Independence," or if on the twenty-second of February, "Georgina," or even "Cherry" like Cherry in "Martin Chuzzlewit"; but I like my own name and birthday best.

Yours truly,
CAROL BIRD

Uncle Jack thought the letter quite right, and did not even smile at her telling the organist so many family items.

The days flew by as they always fly in holiday time, and it was Christmas Eve before anybody knew it. The family festival was quiet and very pleasant, but almost overshadowed by the grander preparations for the next day. Carol and her pretty German nurse, Elfrida, had ransacked books, and introduced so many plans, and plays, and customs, and merry-makings from Germany, and Holland, and England, and a dozen other countries, that you would scarcely have known how or where you were keeping Christmas.

Elfrida had scattered handfuls of seed over the snow in the garden, that the wild birds might have a comfortable breakfast the next morning, and had stuffed bundles of dry grasses in the fireplaces, so that the reindeer of Santa Claus could refresh themselves after their long gallops across country. This was really done only for fun, but it pleased Carol.

And when, after dinner, the whole family had gone to church to see the Christmas decorations, Carol limped out on her crutches, and with Elfrida's help, placed all the family shoes in a row in the upper hall. That was to keep the dear ones from quarreling all through the year. There were Papa's heavy shoes; Mama's pretty slippers next; then Uncle Jack's, Donald's, Paul's, and Hugh's. And at the end of the line her own white woolly slippers. Last, and sweetest of all, like the little children in Austria, she put a lighted candle in her window to guide the dear Christ child, lest He should stumble in the dark night as He passed up the deserted street. That done, she dropped into bed, a rather tired, but happy Christmas fairy.

5.
Some Other Birds
Are Taught to Fly

Before the earliest Ruggles could wake and toot his five-cent tin horn, Mrs. Ruggles was up and stirring about the house, for it was a gala day in the family. Were not all her nine children invited to a dinner party at the Birds' great house? She had been preparing for this grand occasion ever since the receipt of the invitation, which now was in an old photograph frame and hanging under the looking-glass in the most prominent place in the kitchen, where any visitor would see it.

> Birds' Nest, Dec. 17th, 188—
>
> Dear Mrs. Ruggles,
>
> I am going to have a dinner party on Christmas Day, and would like to have all your children come. I want everyone, please, from Sarah Maud to Baby Larry. Mamma says dinner will be at half past five, and the Christmas tree at seven; so you may expect them home at nine o'clock. Wishing you a Merry Christmas and a Happy New Year, I am yours truly,
>
> Carol Bird

Breakfast at the Ruggles' was on the table promptly at seven o'clock, and there was very little of it, too. But it was an excellent day for short rations, though Mrs. Ruggles heaved a sigh as she reflected that the boys, with their India-rubber stomachs, would be just as hungry the day after as if they had never had gone to a dinner party at all.

As soon as the scanty meal was over, she announced the plan of action: "Now Susan, you and Kitty wash up the dishes, so I can get to cutting out Larry's new suit! I'm not satisfied with his clothes, and I thought in the night of a way to make him a dress out of my old red plaid shawl — kind of Scotch style, you know, with the fringe at the bottom.

"Eily, you go find the comb and take the snarls out of the fringe. You little boys clear out from under foot! Clem, you and Con hop into bed with Larry while I wash your underclothes; 't won't take long to dry 'em . . . . Yes, I know it's bothersome, but you can't go into society 'thout taking some trouble, and anyhow I couldn't get round to 'em last night . . . . Sarah Maud, I think 't would be perfectly handsome if you ripped them brass buttons off your uncle's policeman's coat and sewed 'em in a row up the front of your green skirt. Susan, you must iron out yours and Kitty's aprons; and there, I come mighty near forgetting Peory's stockings! I counted the whole lot last night when I was washing 'em, and there ain't but nineteen anyhow you fix 'em, and no nine pairs mates nohow; and I'm not going to have my children wear odd stockings to a company dinner, fetched up as I was! — Eily, you run out and ask Mrs. Cullen to lend me a pair of stockings for Peory, and tell her if she will, Peory'll give Jim half her candy when she gets home. Won't you, Peory?"

Peoria set up a deafening howl at the idea of this projected bargain — a howl so rebellious that her mother started in her direction with flashing eye and uplifted hand; but Mrs. Ruggles let it fall suddenly, saying, "No, I vow I won't hit you Christmas Day, if you drive me crazy. But speak up smart, now, and say whether you'd rather give Jim Cullen half your candy or go bare-legged to the party?"

The matter being put so plainly, Peoria still sniffling, dried her tears, and chose the lesser evil, Clem having hastened the decision by an affectionate wink, that meant he'd go halves with her on his candy.

"That's a lady!" cried her mother. "Now, you young ones that aren't doing anything, play all you want to before noontime, and after you get through eating at twelve o'clock me and Sarah Maud's going to give you sech a washing and combing and dressing as you never had before and never will again likely, and then I'm going to set you down and give you two solid hour's training in manners; and 't won't be no fooling neither."

"All we've got to do's go eat!" grumbled Peter.

"Well, that's enough," responded his mother, "there's more 'n one way of eating, let me tell you, and you've got a heap to learn about it, Peter Ruggles. Land sakes, I wish you children could see the way I was fetched up to eat. I never took a meal in the kitchen before I married Ruggles; but you can't keep up that style with nine young ones 'n' your Pa always off to sea."

The big Ruggleses worked so well, and the little Ruggleses kept from "under foot" so successfully, that by one o'clock nine complete outfits were carefully laid out on the beds.

"Now, Sarah Maud," said Mrs. Ruggles, her face shining with excitement, "we can begin. I've got a boiler and a kettle and a pot of hot water. Peter, you go into the back bedroom, and I'll take Susan, Kitty, Peory, and Cornelius; and Sarah Maud, you take Clem and Eily and Larry, one at a time. Scrub 'em and rinse 'em, or at any rate get as far as you can with 'em, and then I'll finish 'em while you do yourself."

Sarah Maud couldn't have scrubbed with any more decision and force if she had been doing floors, and the little Ruggleses bore it bravely, not from natural heroism, but for the joy that was set before them. And when the clock struck four they were all clothed, and most of them in their right minds, ready for those last touches that always take the most time.

Kitty's red hair was curled in thirty-four ringlets, Sarah Maud's was braided in one pig-tail, and Susan's, Eily's, and Peoria's, in two braids apiece. Then, exciting moment, came linen collars for some and neckties and bows for others — a magnificent green glass pin was sewed into Peter's purple necktie — and Eureka! the Ruggleses were dressed!

A row of seats was then formed directly through the middle of the kitchen. There were not quite chairs enough for ten, since the family had rarely wanted to sit down all at once, somebody's always being out, or in bed, but the wood-box and the coal-hod finished out the line nicely. The children took their places according to age, Sarah Maud at the head and Larry on a board laid across the coal-hod, and Mrs. Ruggles seated herself in front, surveying them proudly as she wiped the sweat of honest toil from her brow.

"Well," she exclaimed, "if I do say so as I shouldn't, I never have seen a cleaner, more stylish mess of children in my life! I do wish Ruggles could look at you for a minute! — Larry Ruggles, how many times have I got to tell you not to keep pulling at your sash? Haven't I told you if it comes untied your top and bottom will part company in the middle, and then where'll you be? — Now look me in the eye, all of you! I've often told you what kind of a family the McGrills were. I've got reason to be proud, goodness knows! Your uncle is on the police force of New York City; you can take up the paper most any day and see his name printed out — James Mc-Grill — and I can't have my children fetched up common, like some folks'; when they go out they've got to have clothes, and learn to act decent! Now I want to see how you're going to behave when you get there tonight. Let's start in at the beginning and act out the whole business. Pile into the bedroom, there, every last one of you and show me how you're going to go into the parlor. This'll be the parlor, and I'll be Mrs. Bird."

The youngsters hustled into the next room in high glee, and Mrs. Ruggles drew herself up in the chair with haughty expression that was not at all like modest Mrs. Bird.

In the small bedroom there was such a clatter that you would have thought a herd of wild cattle had broken loose. The door opened, and they straggled in, all the little ones giggling, with Sarah Maud at the head, looking as if she had been caught in the act of stealing sheep; while Larry, being last in line, seemed to think the door a sort of gate to heaven which would be shut in his face if he didn't get there in time; accordingly he struggled ahead of his elders and disgraced himself by tumbling in head foremost.

Mrs. Ruggles looked severe. "There, I knew you'd do it some such fool way! Now go in there and try it over again, every last one of you, and if Larry can't come in on two legs he can stay home — d' you hear?"

The matter began to assume a graver aspect. The little Ruggleses stopped giggling and backed into the bedroom, issuing presently with lock step, Indian file, a scared and hunted expression on every face.

"No, no, no!" cried Mrs. Ruggles, in despair. "That's worse yet; you look for all the world like a gang of pris'ners! There isn't any style to that. Spread out more, can't you, and act kind of careless like — nobody's goin' ter kill you!" The third time brought deserved success, and the pupils took their seats in the row. "Now, you know," said Mrs. Ruggles impressively, "there aren't enough decent hats to go round, and if there were I don't know as I'd let you wear 'em, for the boys would never think to take 'em off when they got inside — but anyhow, there aren't enough good ones. Now, look me in the eye. You needn't wear any hats, none of you, and when you get into the parlor, and they ask you to lay off your hats, Sarah Maud must speak up and say it was such a pleasant evening and such a short walk that you left your hats at home to save trouble. Now, can you remember?"

All the little Ruggleses shouted, "Yes, ma'am!" in chorus.

"What have *you* got to do with it?" demanded their

mother; "did I tell *you* to say it? Wasn't I talkin' to Sarah Maud?"

The little Ruggleses hung their heads. "Yes, ma'am," they piped, more feebly.

"Now get up, all of you, and try it. Speak up, Sarah Maud."

Sarah Maud's tongue clove to the roof of her mouth. "Quick!"

"Ma thought — it was — such a pleasant hat that we'd — we'd better leave our short walk to home," recited Sarah Maud, in an agony of mental effort.

This was too much for the boys. An earthquake of suppressed giggles swept all along the line.

"Oh, whatever shall I do with you?" moaned the unhappy mother; "I s'pose I've got to teach it to you!" — which she did, word for word, until Sarah Maud thought she could stand on her head and say it backward.

"Now Cornelius, what are *you* going to say to make yourself good company?"

"Me? Dunno!" said Cornelius, turning pale.

"Well, you ain't going to sit there like a bump on a log without saying a word to pay for your vittles, are you? Ask Mrs. Bird how she's feelin' this evening, or if Mr. Bird's having a busy season, or how this kind of weather agrees with him, or somethin' like that — Now we'll make believe we've got to the dinner — that won't be so hard, 'cause you'll have something to do — it's awful bothersome to stand round and act stylish. If they have napkins, Sarah Maud down to Peory may put 'em in their laps, and the rest of you can tuck 'em in your necks. Don't eat with your fingers — don't grab no vittles off one another's plates; don't reach out for nothing, but wait till you're asked, and if you never get asked don't get up and grab it . . . Don't spill nothing on the tablecloth, or like as not Mrs. Bird'll send you away from the table — and I hope she will if you do!

"Now we'll try a few things to see how they'll go! Mr. Clement, do you eat cranberry sauce?"

"Bet your life!" cried Clem, who in the excitement of the moment had not taken in the idea exactly and had mistaken this for an ordinary bosom-of-the-family question.

"Clement McGrill Ruggles, do you mean to tell me that you'd say that at a dinner party? I'll give you one more chance. Mr. Clement, will you take some of the cranberry?"

"Yes ma'am, thank you kindly, if you happen to have any handy."

"Very good, indeed! But they won't give you two tries tonight, you just remember that! — Miss Peory, do you speak for white or dark meat?"

"I'm not partic'lar — anything that nobody else wants, will suit me," answered Peory with her best air.

"First rate! Nobody could speak more genteel than that. Miss Kitty, will you have hard or soft sauce with your pudding?"

"Hard or soft? Oh! A little of both, if you please, and I'm much obliged," said Kitty, bowing with decided ease and grace; at which all the other Ruggleses pointed the finger of shame at her, and Peter grunted expressively, that their meaning might not be mistaken.

"You just stop your grunting, Peter Ruggles; that wasn't greedy, that was all right. I wish I could get it into your heads that it ain't so much what you say, as the way you say it. Eily, you and Larry are too little to train, so you just look at the rest, and do's they do, and the Lord have mercy on you and help you to act decent! Now, is there anything more you'd like to practice?"

"If you tell me one more thing, I can't set up and eat," said Peter, gloomily; "I'm so cram full of manners now I'm ready to bust, without no dinner at all."

"Me too," chimed in Cornelius.

"Well, I'm sorry for you both," rejoined Mrs. Ruggles, sarcastically; "if the amount of manners you've got on hand now troubles you, you're dreadful easy hurt! Now, Sarah Maud, after dinner, you must get up and say, 'I guess we'd better be going'; and if they say, 'Oh, no, sit a while longer,' you can sit; but if they don't say anything, you've got to get up and go. . . . Now have you got that into your head?"

"Well," answered Sarah Maud, mournfully, "seems as if this whole dinner party set right square on top of me! Maybe I could manage my own manners, but to manage nine mannerses is worse'n staying to home!"

"Oh, don't fret," said her mother, good-naturedly, "I guess you'll get along. I wouldn't mind if folks would only say, 'Oh, children will be children'; but they won't. They'll say, 'Land o' goodness, who fetched them children up?' Now it's quarter past five, and you can go now. Remember about the hats, don't all talk ter once, and Susan, lend your handkerchief to Peory. Peter, don't keep wiggling yer tiepin. Cornelius, hold your head up straight — Sarah Maud, don't take your eyes off Larry, and Larry you keep hold of Sarah Maud and do just as she says — and whatever you do, all of you never forget for one second that your mother was a McGrill."

6.
"When the Pie Was Opened, the Birds Began to Sing!"

THE CHILDREN WENT OUT OF THE BACK DOOR QUIETLY, and were presently lost to sight, Sarah Maud slipping and stumbling along absent-mindedly, as she recited rapidly under her breath, "Itwassuchapleasantevenin'n'suchashortwalk, thatwethoughtwe'dleaveourhatstohome."

Peter rang the doorbell, and presently a servant admitted them, and, whispering something in Sarah's ear, drew her downstairs into the kitchen. The other Ruggleses stood in horror-stricken groups as the door closed behind their commanding officer; but there was no time for reflection, for a voice from above was heard, saying, "Come right upstairs please!"

Accordingly, they walked upstairs, and Elfrida, the nurse, ushered them into a room more splendid than anything they had ever seen. But, oh woe! Where was Sarah Maud? And was it Fate that Mrs. Bird should say, at once, "Did you lay your hats in the hall?" Peter felt himself elected by circumstance the head of the family, and, casting one imploring look at tongue-tied Susan, standing next to him, said huskily, "It was so very pleasant — that — that — " "That we hadn't good hats enough to go round," put in little Susan bravely, to help him out, and then froze with horror that the ill-fated words had slipped off her tongue.

However, Mrs. Bird said, pleasantly, "Of course you wouldn't wear hats such a short distance — I forgot when I asked. Now will you come right in to Miss Carol's room? She is so anxious to see you."

Just then Sarah Maud came up the backstairs, so radiant with joy from her secret interview with the cook that Peter could have pinched her with a clear conscience, and Carol gave them a joyful welcome. "But where is Baby Larry?" she cried, looking over the group with searching eye. "Didn't he come?"

"Larry! Larry!" Good gracious, where was Larry? They were all sure that he had come in with them, for Susan said she remembered scolding him for tripping over the doormat. Uncle Jack laughed. "Are you sure there were nine of you?" he asked, jokingly.

"I think so, sir," said Peoria, timidly, "but anyhow, there was Larry," and she showed signs of weeping.

"Oh, well, cheer up!" cried Uncle Jack. "I guess he's not lost — only mislaid. I'll go and find him before you can say Jack Robinson!"

"I'll go, too, if you please sir," said Sarah Maud, "for it was my place to mind him, an' if he's lost I can't relish my vittles!"

The other Ruggleses stood rooted to the floor. If this was a dinner party, why were such things ever spoken of as festive occasions?

Sarah Maud went out through the hall, calling, "Larry! Larry!" and without any interval of suspense a little voice piped up from below, "Here I be!"

The truth was that Larry, being deserted by his natural guardian, dropped behind the rest, and wriggled into the hat tree to wait for her, having no notion of walking unprotected into the jaws of a dinner party. Finding that she did not come, he tried to crawl from his refuge and call somebody, when — dark and dreadful ending to a tragic day — he found that he was too much intertwined with umbrellas and canes to move a single step. He was afraid to yell, but the sound of Sarah Maud's familiar voice, some seconds later, carried him upstairs, and soon had him in breathless fits of laughter, while Carol so made the other Ruggleses forget themselves that they were presently talking like accomplished diners-out.

Carol's bed had been moved into the farthest corner of the room, and she was propped up on it, dressed in a wonderful soft white robe. Her golden hair fell in fluffy curls over her white forehead and neck, her cheeks flushed delicately, her eyes beamed with joy, and the children told their mother afterward that she looked as beautiful as the angels in the picture books.

There was a great bustle behind a huge screen in another part of the room, and at half past five this was taken away, and the Christmas dinner table stood revealed. What a wonderful sight it was to the Ruggles children! It blazed with tall, colored candles, it gleamed with glass and silver, it blushed with flowers, it groaned with good things to eat. So it was not strange that the Ruggleses, forgetting that their mother was a McGrill, shrieked in admiration of the fairy spectacle. But Larry's behavior was the most disgraceful, for he went at once to a high chair, climbed up like a squirrel, gave a look at the turkey, clapped his hands in ecstasy, rested his fat arms on the table, and cried with joy, "I beat the hull lot o'yer!" Carol laughed until she cried, giving orders meanwhile —"Uncle Jack, please sit at the head, Sarah Maud at the foot, and that will leave four on each side. Mamma is going to help Elfrida, so you will not have to look after each other, but just have a good time."

A sprig of holly lay by each plate, and nothing would do but each little Ruggles must leave his seat and have it pinned on by Carol, and as each course was served, one of them pleaded to take something to her. There was hurrying to and fro, for it is quite a difficult matter to serve a Christmas dinner so far away from the down-stairs kitchen. But if it had been necessary to carry every dish up a rope ladder the servants would gladly have done so — both for Carol's sake, and the joy and gusto with which the Ruggles children ate up the food. There were turkey and chicken, with delicious gravy and stuff-ing, and there were half a dozen vegetables, with cran-berry jelly, and celery, and pickles; and as for the elegant way in which these delicacies were served, the Ruggleses never forgot it as long as they lived.

Peter nudged Kitty, who sat next to him, and said, "Look! Every feller's got his own partic'lar butter; I s'pose that's to show you can eat that and no more. No, it ain't either, for that pig of a Peory's just getting an-other helping!"

"Yes," whispered Kitty, "and the napkins are marked with big red letters! I wonder if that's so nobody'll nip 'em; an' oh, Peter, look at the pictures sticking right on to the dishes! Did you *ever*?"

"The plums is all took out o'my cramb'ry sauce an' it's friz to a stiff jell," whispered Peoria, in wild excitement.

"Hi — yah! I got a wishbone!" sang Larry, regardless of Sarah Maud's frown. She asked to have his seat changed, giving as excuse that he generally sat beside her, and would "feel strange"; the true reason was that she desired to kick him gently, under the table, whenever he passed beyond what might be termed "the McGrill line."

"I declare to goodness," murmured Susan, on the other side, "there's so much to look at I can't scarcely eat anything!"

"Bet your life I can!" said Peter, who had kept one servant busily employed ever since he sat down; for, luckily, no one was asked by Uncle Jack whether he would have a second helping, but the dishes were quietly passed under their noses again and again, and not a single Ruggles refused anything that was offered.

Then, when Carol and Uncle Jack saw that more turkey was a physical impossibility, the dessert was brought in — a dessert that would have frightened a strong man after such a dinner as had preceded it! Not so the Ruggleses!

There were plum pudding, mince pie, and ice cream; and there were nuts, and raisins, and oranges. Kitty chose ice cream, explaining that she knew it "by sight, though she hadn't ever tasted any"; but all the rest took the entire variety, without any regard to consequences.

"My dear child," whispered Uncle Jack, as he took Carol an orange, "there is no doubt about the necessity of this feast, but I do advise you after this to have them twice a year, or quarterly perhaps, for the way these children eat is positively dangerous; I assure you I tremble for that terrible Peoria. I'm going to run races with her after dinner."

"Never mind," laughed Carol; "let them have enough for once; and I shall invite them oftener next year."

The feast being over, the Ruggleses leaned back in their chairs and the table was cleared in a trice. Then a door was opened into the next room, and there, in a corner facing Carol's bed, which had been wheeled as close as possible, stood the brilliantly lighted Christmas tree, glittering with gilded walnuts and tiny silver balloons, and wreathed with snowy chains of popcorn. The presents had been bought mostly with Carol's story money, and were selected after long consultations with Mrs. Bird. Each girl had a blue knitted hood, and each boy a red crocheted scarf, all made by Mamma, Carol, and Elfrida. Then every girl had a pretty plaid dress of a different color, and every boy a warm coat of the right size.

Here the useful presents stopped. Carol had pleaded to give them something "for fun." "I know they need clothes," she had said, when they were talking over the matter just after Thanksgiving, "but they don't care much for them, after all. Now, Papa, won't you *please* give me the money you would spend on presents for me, so that I can buy presents for the Ruggleses?"

"You can have both," said Mr. Bird promptly. "Is there any need of my little girl's going without her own Christmas, I should like to know? Spend all the money you like."

"But that isn't the thing," objected Carol, nestling close to her father. "The presents wouldn't really be from me, then, and haven't I almost everything already? I'm the happiest girl in the world this year, with Uncle Jack and Donald at home. Why won't you let me do it? You never look half as happy when you are getting your presents as when you are giving us ours. Now, Papa, say 'yes,' or I shall have to be very firm and disagreeable with you!"

"Very well, Your Highness, I surrender. But a bronze figure of Santa Claus, and in the little round belly that shakes when he laughs like a bowl of jelly, is a wonderful clock — oh, you would never give it up if you could see it!"

"Nonsense," laughed Carol. "As I never have to get up to breakfast, nor go to bed, nor catch trains, I think my old clock will do very well! Now, Mamma, what were you going to give me?"

"Oh, I hadn't decided. A few more books, and a gold thimble, and a smelling bottle, and a music box, perhaps."

"Poor Carol," laughed the child, merrily, "she can afford to give up these lovely things, for there will still be left Uncle Jack, and Donald, and Paul, and Hugh, and Uncle Rob, and Aunt Elsie, and a dozen other people to fill her Christmas stocking!"

So Carol had her way, as she generally did, and Sarah Maud had a set of Louisa May Alcott's books, and Peter a modest silver watch, Cornelius a tool chest, Clement a doghouse for his lame puppy, Larry a magnificent Noah's ark, and each of the little girls a beautiful doll.

You can well believe that everybody was very merry! All the family, from Mr. Bird down to the cook, said that they had never seen so much happiness in the space of three hours! But it had to end, as all things do. The candles flickered and went out. The tree shorn of gifts was left alone with just its gilded ornaments. Mrs. Bird had Elfrida lead the children downstairs at half past eight, thinking that Carol looked tired.

"Now, my darling, you have done quite enough for one day," said Mrs. Bird, getting Carol into her nightgown. "If you were to feel worse tomorrow that would be a sad ending to such a charming evening."

"Oh, wasn't it a lovely, lovely time," sighed Carol. "From first to last, everything was just right. I shall never forget Larry's face when he looked at the turkey; nor Peter's when he saw his watch; nor that sweet, sweet Kitty's smile when she kissed her doll; nor the tears in poor Sarah Maud's eyes when she thanked me for her books; nor — "

"But we mustn't talk any longer about it tonight," said Mrs. Bird, anxiously. "You are too tired, dear."

"I am not so very tired, Mamma. I have felt well all day; not a bit of pain anywhere. Perhaps this has done me good."

"Perhaps," Mrs. Bird smiled. "It was a merry time. Now, may I close the door and leave you alone, dear? Papa and I will steal in softly by and by to see if you are all right; but I think you need to be very quiet."

"Oh, I'm willing to stay alone; but I am not sleepy yet, and I am going to hear the music, you know."

"Yes, I have opened the window a little, and put the screen in front of it, so that you won't feel a draft."

"Can I have the shutters open? And won't you turn my bed a little, please? This morning I woke ever so early, and one bright, beautiful star shone in that eastern window. I never noticed it before, and I thought of the

Star in the East, that guided the wise men to the place where the baby Jesus was. Good night, Mamma. Such a happy, happy day!"

"Good night, my precious Christmas Carol — mother's own Christmas child."

"Bend your head a minute, Mother dear," whispered Carol, calling her mother back. "Mamma, dear, I do think that we have kept Christ's birthday this time just as He would like it. Don't you?"

"I am sure of it," said Mrs. Bird softly.

7.
The Birdling Flies Away

THE RUGGLESES HAD FINISHED A LAST ROMP IN THE library with Paul and Hugh, and Uncle Jack had taken them home and stayed a while to chat with Mrs. Ruggles, who opened the door for them, her face all aglow with excitement and delight. When Kitty and Clem showed her the oranges and nuts that they had kept for her, she astonished them by saying that at six o'clock Mrs. Bird had sent her in the finest dinner she had ever seen in her life; and not only that, but a piece of dress goods that must have cost a dollar a yard if it cost a cent.

As Uncle Jack went down the little porch he looked back into the window for a last glimpse of the family, as the children gathered about their mother, showing their beautiful presents again and again, and then upward to a window in the great house yonder. "A little child shall lead them," he thought. "Well, if — if anything ever happens to Carol, I will take the Ruggleses under my wing."

"Softly, Uncle Jack," whispered the boys, as he walked into the library a little while later. "We are listening to the music in the church. The choir sang 'Carol, brothers, carol,' a while ago, and now we think the organist is beginning to play 'My ain countree' for Carol."

"I hope she hears it," said Mrs. Bird, "but they are very late tonight, and she may be asleep. It is almost ten o'clock."

The boy soprano, clad in white surplice, stood in the organ loft. The light shone full upon him, and his pale face, with its serious blue eyes, looked paler than usual. Perhaps it was something in the tender trill of the voice, or in the sweet words, but there were tears in many eyes, both in the church and in the big house next door.

> "I am far frae my hame,
>   I am weary aften whiles
> For the langed-for hame-bringing',
>   An' my Faether's welcome smiles;
> An' I'll ne'er be fu' content,
>   Until my e'en do see
> The golden gates o'heaven
>   In my ain countree."

There were tears in many eyes, but not in Carol's. The "wee birdie" in the great house had flown to its "home nest." Carol had fallen asleep! The loving heart had quietly ceased to beat.

So sad an ending to a happy day! And yet Carol's mother, even in the freshness of her grief, was glad that her darling had slipped away on the loveliest day of her life, out of its glad content, into everlasting peace.

She was glad that she had gone as she had come, on

68

the wings of song, when Christmas was brimming over with joy; glad of every grateful smile, of every joyous burst of laughter, of every loving thought and word and deed that the last day had brought.

Sadness reigned, it is true, in the little house behind the garden.

One day poor Sarah Maud, with a courage born of despair, threw on her hood and shawl, walked straight to a certain house a mile away, up the marble steps into good Dr. Bartol's office.

"Oh, sir," she cried, "it was me an' our children that went to Miss Carol's last dinner party, an' if we made her worse we can't never be happy again!" Then the kind old gentleman took her hand in his and told her to dry her tears, for neither she nor any of her flock had hastened Carol's flight — indeed, he said that had it not been for the strong hopes and wishes that filled her tired heart, Carol could not have stayed long enough to keep that last merry Christmas with her dear ones.

And so the old years, filled with memories, die, one after another, and the new years, bright with hopes, are born to take their places; but Carol lives again in every chime of Christmas bells that peal glad tidings and in every Christmas anthem sung by childish voices.

A Christmas Dream
and
How It Came True

Louisa May Alcott

I'M SO TIRED OF CHRISTMAS I WISH THERE NEVER WOULD be another one!" exclaimed a discontented-looking little girl, as she sat idly watching her mother arrange a pile of gifts two days before they were to be given.

"Why, Effie, what a dreadful thing to say! You are as bad as old Scrooge; and I'm afraid something will happen to you, as it did to him, if you don't care for dear Christmas," answered mamma, almost dropping the silver horn she was filling with delicious candies.

"Who was Scrooge? What happened to him?" asked Effie, with a glimmer of interest in her listless face, as she picked out the sourest lemon-drop she could find; for nothing sweet suited her just then.

"He was one of Dickens's best people, and you can read the charming story some day. He hated Christmas until a strange dream showed him how dear and beautiful it was, and made a better man of him."

"I shall read it; for I like dreams, and have a great many curious ones myself. But they don't keep me from being tired of Christmas," said Effie, poking discontentedly among the sweeties for something worth eating.

"Why are you tired of what should be the happiest time of all the year?" asked mamma, anxiously.

"Perhaps I shouldn't be if I had something new. But it is always the same, and there isn't any more surprise about it. I always find heaps of goodies in my stocking. Don't like some of them, and soon get tired of those I do like. We always have a great dinner, and I eat too much, and feel ill next day. Then there is a Christmas tree somewhere, with a doll on top, or a stupid old Santa Claus, and children dancing and screaming over bonbons and toys that break, and shiny things that are of

73

no use. Really, mamma, I've had so many Christmases all alike that I don't think I *can* bear another one." And Effie laid herself flat on the sofa, as if the mere idea was too much for her.

Her mother laughed at her despair, but was sorry to see her little girl so discontented, when she had everything to make her happy, and had known but ten Christmas days.

"Suppose we don't give you *any* presents at all — how would that suit you?" asked mamma, anxious to please her spoiled child.

"I should like one large and splendid one, and one dear little one, to remember some very nice person by," said Effie, who was a fanciful little body, full of odd whims and notions, which her friends loved to gratify, regardless of time, trouble, or money; for she was the last of three little girls, and very dear to all the family.

"Well, my darling, I will see what I can do to please you, and not say a word until all is ready. If I could only get a new idea to start with!" And mamma went on tying up her pretty bundles with a thoughtful face, while Effie strolled to the window to watch the rain that kept her in-doors and made her dismal.

"Seems to me poor children have better times than rich ones. I can't go out, and there is a girl about my age splashing along, without any maid to fuss about rubbers and cloaks and umbrellas and colds. I wish I was a beggar-girl."

"Would you like to be hungry, cold, and ragged, to beg all day, and sleep on an ash-heap at night?" asked mamma, wondering what would come next.

74

"Cinderella did, and had a nice time in the end. This girl out here has a basket of scraps on her arm, and a big old shawl all round her, and doesn't seem to care a bit, though the water runs out of the toes of her boots. She goes paddling along, laughing at the rain, and eating a cold potato as if it tasted nicer than the chicken and ice-cream I had for dinner. Yes, I do think poor children are happier than rich ones."

"So do I, sometimes. At the Orphan Asylum today I saw two dozen merry little souls who have no parents, no home, and no hope of Christmas beyond a stick of candy or a cake. I wish you had been there to see how happy they were, playing with the old toys some richer children had sent them."

"You may give them all mine; I'm so tired of them I never want to see them again," said Effie, turning from the window to the pretty baby-house full of everything a child's heart could desire.

"I will, and let you begin again with something you will not tire of, if I can only find it." And mamma knit her brows trying to discover some grand surprise for this child who didn't care for Christmas.

Nothing more was said then; and wandering off to the library, Effie found "A Christmas Carol," and, curling herself up in the sofa corner, read it all before tea. Some of it she did not understand; but she laughed and cried over many parts of the charming story, and felt better without knowing why.

All the evening she thought of poor Tiny Tim, Mrs. Cratchit with the pudding, and the stout old gentleman who danced so gayly that "his legs twinkled in the air." Presently bed-time arrived.

75

"Come now, and toast your feet," said Effie's nurse, "while I do your pretty hair and tell stories."

"I'll have a fairy tale tonight, a very interesting one," commanded Effie, as she put on her blue silk wrapper and little fur-lined slippers to sit before the fire and have her long curls brushed.

So Nursey told her best tales; and when at last the child lay down under her lace curtains, her head was full of a curious jumble of Christmas elves, poor children, snow-storms, sugar-plums, and surprises. So it is no wonder that she dreamed all night; and this was the dream, which she never quite forgot.

She found herself sitting on a stone, in the middle of a great field, all alone. The snow was falling fast, a bitter wind whistled by, and night was coming on. She felt hungry, cold, and tired, and did not know where to go nor what to do.

"I wanted to be a beggar-girl, and now I am one; but I don't like it, and wish somebody would come and take care of me. I don't know who I am, and I think I must be lost," thought Effie, with the curious interest one takes in one's self in dreams.

But the more she thought about it, the more bewildered she felt. Faster fell the snow, colder blew the wind, darker grew the night; and poor Effie made up her mind that she was quite forgotten and left to freeze alone. The tears were chilled on her cheeks, her feet felt like icicles, and her heart died within her, so hungry, frightened, and forlorn was she. Laying her head on her knees, she gave herself up for lost, and sat there with the great flakes fast turning her to a little white mound, when suddenly the sound of music reached her, and starting up, she looked and listened with all her eyes and ears.

Far away a dim light shone, and a voice was heard singing. She tried to run toward the welcome glimmer, but could not stir, and stood like a small statue of expectation while the light drew nearer, and the sweet words of the song grew clearer.

"From our happy home
  Through the world we roam
One week in all the year,
  Making winter spring
  With the joy we bring
For Christmas-tide is here.

"Now the eastern star
  Shines from afar
To light the poorest home;
  Hearts warmer grow,
  Gifts freely flow,
For Christmas-tide has come.

"Now gay trees rise
  Before young eyes,
Abloom with tempting cheer;
  Blithe voices sing.
  And blithe bells ring,
For Christmas-tide is here.

"Oh, happy chime,
  Oh, blessed time,
That draws us all so near!

          'Welcome, dear day,'
          All creatures say,
       For Christmas-tide is here."

A child's voice sang, a child's hand carried the little
candle; and in the circle of soft light it shed, Effie saw
a pretty child coming to her through the night and snow.
A rosy, smiling creature, wrapped in white fur, with a
wreath of green and scarlet holly on its shining hair, the
magic candle in one hand, and the other outstretched
as if to shower gifts and warmly press all other hands.

Effie forgot to speak as this bright vision came nearer,
leaving no trace of footsteps in the snow, only lighting
the way with its little candle, and filling the air with the
music of its song.

"Dear child, you are lost, and I have come to find
you," said the stranger, taking Effie's cold hands in his,
with a smile like sunshine, while every holly berry glowed
like a little fire.

"Do you know me?" asked Effie, feeling no fear, but
a great gladness, at his coming.

"I know all children, and go to find them; for this is
my holiday, and I gather them from all parts of the
world to be merry with me once a year."

"Are you an angel?" asked Effie, looking for the wings.

"No; I am a Christmas spirit, and live with my mates
in a pleasant place, getting ready for our holiday, when
we are let out to roam about the world, helping to make
this a happy time for all who will let us in. Will you come
and see how we work?"

"I will go anywhere with you. Don't leave me again,"
cried Effie, gladly.

"First I will make you comfortable. That is what we love to do. You are cold, and you shall be warm; hungry, and I will feed you; sorrowful, and I will make you gay."

With a wave of his candle all three miracles were wrought — for the snow-flakes turned to a white fur cloak and hood on Effie's head and shoulders; a bowl of hot soup came sailing to her lips, and vanished when she had eagerly drunk the last drop; and suddenly the dismal field changed to a new world so full of wonders that all her troubles were forgotten in a minute.

Bells were ringing so merrily that it was hard to keep from dancing. Green garlands hung on the walls, and every tree was a Christmas tree full of toys, and blazing with candles that never went out.

In one place many little spirits sewed like mad on warm clothes, turning off work faster than any sewing-machine ever invented, and great piles were made ready to be sent to poor people. Other busy creatures packed money into purses, and wrote checks which they sent flying away on the wind — a lovely kind of snow-storm to fall into a world below full of poverty.

Older and graver spirits were looking over piles of little books, in which the records of the past year were kept, telling how different people had spent it, and what sort of gifts they deserved. Some got peace, some disappointment, some remorse and sorrow, some great joy and hope. The rich had generous thoughts sent them; the poor, gratitude and contentment. Children had more love and duty to parents; and parents renewed patience, wisdom, and satisfaction for and in their children. No one was forgotten.

"Please tell me what splendid place this is?" asked

Effie, as soon as she could collect her wits after the first look at all these astonishing things.

"This is the Christmas world; and here we work all the year round, never tired of getting ready for the happy day. See, these are the saints just setting off, for some have far to go, and the children must not be disappointed."

As he spoke the spirit pointed to four gates, out of which four great sleighs were just driving, laden with toys, while a jolly old Santa Claus sat in the middle of each, drawing on his mittens and tucking up his wraps for a long cold drive.

"Why, I thought there was only one Santa Claus, and even he was a humbug," cried Effie, astonished at the sight.

"Never give up your faith in the sweet old stories, even after you come to see that they are only the pleasant shadow of a lovely truth."

Just then the sleighs went off with a great jingling of bells and pattering of reindeer hoofs, while all the spirits gave a cheer that was heard in the lower world, where people said, "Hear the stars sing."

"I never will say there isn't any Santa Claus again. Now, show me more."

"You will like to see this place, I think, and may learn something here perhaps."

The spirit smiled as he led the way to a little door, through which Effie peeped into a world of dolls. Baby-houses were in full blast, with dolls of all sorts going on like live people. Waxen ladies sat in their parlors elegantly dressed; some dolls cooked in the kitchens; nurses walked out with the bits of dollies; and the streets were full of tin soldiers marching, wooden horses prancing, express wagons rumbling; and little men hurrying to and fro. Shops were there, and tiny people buying legs of mutton, pounds of tea, mites of clothes, and everything dolls use or wear or want.

But presently she saw that in some ways the dolls improved upon the manners and customs of human beings, and she watched eagerly to learn why they did these things. A fine Paris doll driving in her carriage took up another doll who was hobbling along with a basket of clean clothes, and carried her to her journey's end, as if it were the proper thing to do. Another interesting china lady took off her comfortable red cloak and put it round a poor wooden creature done up in a paper shift, and so badly painted that its face would have sent some babies into fits.

"Seems to me I once knew a rich girl who didn't give her things to poor girls. I wish I could remember who she was, and tell her to be as kind as that china doll," said Effie, much touched at the sweet way the pretty creature wrapped up the poor fright, and then ran off in her little gray gown to buy a shiny fowl stuck on a wooden platter for her invalid mother's dinner.

"We recall these things to people's minds by dreams. I think the girl you speak of won't forget this one." And the spirit smiled, as if he enjoyed some joke which she did not see.

A little bell rang as she looked, and away scampered the children into the red-and-green school-house with the roof that lifted up, so one could see how nicely they sat at their desks with mites of books, or drew on the inch-square blackboards with crumbs of chalk.

"They know their lessons very well, and are as still as mice. We make a great racket at our school, and get bad marks every day. I shall tell the girls they had better mind what they do, or their dolls will be better scholars than they are," said Effie, much impressed, as she peeped in and saw no rod in the hand of the little mistress, who looked up and shook her head at the intruder, as if begging her to go away before the order of the school was disturbed.

Effie retired at once, but could not resist one look in the window of a fine mansion, where the family were at dinner, the children behaved so well at table, and never grumbled a bit when their mamma said they could not have any more fruit.

"Now, show me something else," she said, as they came again to the low door that led out of Doll-land.

"You have seen how we prepare for Christmas; let me show you where we love best to send our good and happy gifts," answered the spirit, giving her his hand again.

"I know. I've seen ever so many," began Effie, thinking of her own Christmases.

"No, you have never seen what I will show you. Come away, and remember what you see tonight."

Like a flash that bright world vanished, and Effie found herself in a part of the city she had never seen before. It was far away from the gayer places, where every store was brilliant with lights and full of pretty things, and every house wore a festival air, while people hurried to and fro with merry greetings. It was down among the dingy streets where the poor lived, and where there was no making ready for Christmas.

Hungry women looked in at the shabby shops, longing

to buy meat and bread, but empty pockets forbade. Tipsy men drank up their wages in the bar-rooms; and in many cold dark chambers little children huddled under the thick blankets, trying to forget their misery in sleep.

No nice dinners filled the air with savory smells, no gay trees dropped toys and bonbons into eager hands, no little stockings hung in rows beside the chimney-piece ready to be filled, no happy sounds of music, gay voices, and dancing feet were heard; and there were no signs of Christmas anywhere.

"Don't they have any in this place?" asked Effie, shivering, as she held fast the spirit's hand, following where he led her.

"We come to bring it. Let me show you our best workers." And the spirit pointed to some sweet-faced men and women who came stealing into the poor houses, working such beautiful miracles that Effie could only stand and watch.

Some slipped money into the empty pockets, and sent the happy mothers to buy all the comforts they needed; others led the drunken men out of temptation, and took them home to find safer pleasures there. Fires were kindled on cold hearths, tables spread as if by magic, and warm clothes wrapped round shivering limbs. Flowers suddenly bloomed in the chambers of the sick; old people found themselves remembered; sad hearts were consoled by a tender word, and wicked ones softened by the story of Him who forgave all sin.

But the sweetest work was for the children; and Effie held her breath to watch these human fairies hang up and fill the little stockings without which a child's Christmas is not perfect, putting in things that once she would have thought very humble presents, but which now seemed beautiful and precious because these poor babies had nothing.

"That is so beautiful! I wish I could make merry Christmas as these good people do, and be loved and thanked as they are," said Effie, softly, as she watched the busy men and women do their work and steal away without thinking of any reward but their own satisfaction.

"You can if you will. I have shown you the way. Try it, and see how happy your own holiday will be hereafter."

As he spoke, the spirit seemed to put his arms about her, and vanished with a kiss.

"Oh, stay and show me more!" cried Effie, trying to hold him fast.

"Darling, wake up, and tell me why you are smiling in your sleep," said a voice in her ear; and opening her eyes, there was mamma bending over her, and morning sunshine streaming into the room.

"Are they all gone? Did you hear the bells? Wasn't it splendid?" she asked, rubbing her eyes, and looking about her for the pretty child who was so real and sweet.

"You have been dreaming at a great rate — talking in your sleep, laughing, and clapping your hands as if you were cheering some one. Tell me what was so splendid," said mamma, smoothing the tumbled hair and lifting up the sleepy head.

Then, while she was being dressed, Effie told her dream, and Nursey thought it very wonderful; but mamma smiled to see how curiously things the child had thought, read, heard, and seen through the day were mixed up in her sleep.

"The spirit said I could work lovely miracles if I tried; but I don't know how to begin, for I have no magic candle to make feasts appear, and light up groves of Christmas trees, as he did," said Effie, sorrowfully.

"Yes you have. We will do it! we will do it!" And clapping her hands, mamma suddenly began to dance all over the room as if she had lost her wits.

"How? how? You must tell me, mamma," cried Effie, dancing after her, and ready to believe anything possible when she remembered the adventures of the past night.

"I've got it! I've got it! — the new idea. A splendid one, if I can only carry it out!" And mamma waltzed the little girl round till her curls flew wildly in the air, while Nursey laughed as if she would die.

"Tell me! tell me!" shrieked Effie.

"No, no; it is a surprise — a grand surprise for Christmas day!" sung mamma, evidently charmed with her happy thought. "Now, come to breakfast; for we must work like bees if we want to play spirits tomorrow. You and Nursey will go out shopping, and get heaps of things, while I arrange matters behind the scenes."

They were running downstairs as mamma spoke, and Effie called out breathlessly —

"It won't be a surprise; for I know you are going to ask some poor children here, and have a tree or something. It won't be like my dream; for they had ever so many trees, and more children than we can find anywhere."

"There will be no tree, no party, no dinner, in this house at all, and no presents for you. Won't that be a surprise?" And mamma laughed at Effie's bewildered face.

"Do it. I shall like it, I think; and I won't ask any questions, so it will all burst upon me when the time comes," she said; and she ate her breakfast thoughtfully, for this really would be a new sort of Christmas.

All that morning Effie trotted after Nursey in and out of shops, buying dozens of barking dogs, woolly lambs, and squeaking birds; tiny tea-sets, gay picture-books, mittens and hoods, dolls and candy. Parcel after parcel was sent home; but when Effie returned she saw no trace of them, though she peeped everywhere. Nursey chuckled, but wouldn't give a hint, and went out again in the afternoon with a long list of more things to buy; while Effie wandered forlornly about the house, missing the usual merry stir that went before the Christmas dinner and the evening fun.

As for mamma, she was quite invisible all day, and came in at night so tired that she could only lie on the sofa to rest, smiling as if some very pleasant thought made her happy in spite of weariness.

"Is the surprise going on all right?" asked Effie, anxiously; for it seemed an immense time to wait till another evening came.

"Beautifully! Better than I expected; for several of my good friends are helping, or I couldn't have done as I wish. I know you will like it, dear, and long remember this new way of making Christmas merry."

Mamma gave her a very tender kiss, and Effie went to bed.

The next day was a very strange one; for when she woke there was no stocking to examine, no pile of gifts under her napkin, no one said, "Merry Christmas!" to her, and the dinner was just as usual to her. Mamma vanished again, and Nursey kept wiping her eyes and saying: "The dear things! It's the prettiest idea I ever heard of. No one but your blessed ma could have done it."

"Do stop, Nursey, or I shall go crazy because I don't know the secret!" cried Effie, more than once; and she kept her eye on the clock, for at seven in the evening the surprise was to come off.

The longed-for hour arrived at last, and the child was too excited to ask questions when Nursey put on her cloak and hood, led her to the carriage, and they drove away, leaving their house the one dark and silent one in the row.

"I feel like the girls in the fairy tales who are led off to strange places and see fine things," said Effie, in a whisper, as they jingled through the gay streets.

"Ah, my deary, it *is* like a fairy tale, I do assure you, and you will see finer things than most children will tonight. Steady, now, and do just as I tell you, and don't say one word whatever you see," answered Nursey, quite quivering with excitement as she patted a large box in her lap, and nodded and laughed with twinkling eyes.

They drove into a dark yard, and Effie was led through a back door to a little room, where Nursey coolly proceeded to take off not only Effie's cloak and hood but her dress and shoes also. Effie stared and bit her lips, but kept still until out of the box came a little white fur coat and boots, a wreath of holly leaves and berries, and a candle with a frill of gold paper round it. A long "Oh!" escaped her then; and when she was dressed and saw herself in the glass, she started back, exclaiming, "Why, Nursey, I look like the spirit in my dream!"

"So you do; and that's the part you are to play, my pretty! Now whist, while I blind your eyes and put you in your place."

"Shall I be afraid?" whispered Effie, full of wonder; for as they went out she heard the sound of many voices, the tramp of many feet, and, in spite of the bandage, was sure a great light shone upon her when she stopped.

"You needn't be; I shall stand close by, and your ma will be there."

After the handkerchief was tied about her eyes, Nursey led Effie up some steps, and placed her on a high platform, where something like leaves touched her head, and the soft snap of lamps seemed to fill the air.

Music began as soon as Nursey clapped her hands, the voices outside sounded nearer, and the tramp was evidently coming up the stairs.

"Now, my precious, look and see how you and your dear ma have made a merry Christmas for them that needed it!"

Off went the bandage; and for a minute Effie really did think she was asleep again, for she actually stood in "a grove of Christmas trees," all gay and shining as in her vision. Twelve on a side, in two rows down the room, stood the little pines, each on its low table; and behind Effie a taller one rose to the roof, hung with wreaths of popcorn, apples, oranges, horns of candy, and cakes of

88

all sorts, from sugary hearts to gingerbread Jumbos. On the smaller trees she saw many of her own discarded toys and those Nursey bought, as well as heaps that seemed to have rained down straight from that delight-ful Christmas country where she felt as if she was again.

"How splendid! Who is it for? What is that noise? Where is mamma?" cried Effie, pale with pleasure and surprise, as she stood looking down the brilliant little street from her high place.

Before Nursey could answer, the doors at the lower end flew open, and in marched twenty-four little blue-gowned orphan girls, singing sweetly, until amazement changed the song to cries of joy and wonder as the shining spectacle appeared. While they stood staring with round eyes at the wilderness of pretty things about them, mamma stepped up beside Effie, and holding her hand fast to give her courage, told the story of the dream in a few simple words, ending in this way:

"So my little girl wanted to be a Christmas spirit too, and make this a happy day for those who had not as many pleasures and comforts as she has. She likes sur-prises, and we planned this for you all. She shall play the good fairy, and give each of you something from this tree, after which every one will find her own name on a small tree, and can go to enjoy it in her own way. March by, my dears, and let us fill your hands."

Nobody told them to do it, but all the hands were clapped heartily before a single child stirred; then one by one they came to look up wonderingly at the pretty giver of the feast as she leaned down to offer them great yellow oranges, red apples, bunches of grapes, bonbons, and cakes, till all were gone, and a double row of smiling faces turned toward her as the children filed back to their places in the orderly way they had been taught.

Then each was led to her own tree by the good ladies who had helped mamma with all their hearts; and the happy hubbub that arose would have satisfied even Santa Claus himself — shrieks of joy, dances of delight, laughter and tears (for some tender little things could not bear so much pleasure at once, and sobbed with mouths full of candy and hands full of toys). How they ran to show one another the new treasures! how they peeped and tasted, pulled and pinched, until the air was full of queer noises, the floor covered with papers, and the little trees left bare of all but candles!

"I don't think heaven can be any gooder than this," sighed one small girl, as she looked about her in a blissful maze, holding her full apron with one hand, while she luxuriously carried sugar-plums to her mouth with the other.

"Is that a truly angel up there?" asked another, fascinated by the little white figure with the wreath on its shining hair, who in some mysterious way had been the cause of all this merry-making.

"I wish I dared to go and kiss her for this splendid party," said a lame child, leaning on her crutch, as she stood near the steps, wondering how it seemed to sit in a mother's lap, as Effie was doing, while she watched the happy scene before her.

Effie heard her, and remembering Tiny Tim, ran down and put her arms about the pale child, kissing the wistful face, as she said sweetly, "You may; but mamma deserves the thanks. She did it all; I only dreamed about it."

Lame Katy felt as if "a truly angel" was embracing her, and could only stammer out her thanks, while the other children ran to see the pretty spirit, and touch her soft dress, until she stood in a crowd of blue gowns laughing as they held up their gifts for her to see and admire.

Mamma leaned down and whispered one word to the older girls; and suddenly they all took hands to dance round Effie, singing as they skipped.

It was a pretty sight, and the ladies found it hard to break up the happy revel; but it was late for small people, and too much fun is a mistake. So the girls fell into line, and marched before Effie and mamma again, to say good-night with such grateful little faces that the eyes of those who looked grew dim with tears. Mamma kissed every one; and many a hungry childish heart felt as if the touch of those tender lips was their best gift. Effie shook so many small hands that her own tingled; and when Katy came she pressed a small doll into Effie's hand, whispering, "You didn't have a single present, and we had lots. Do keep that; it's the prettiest thing I got."

"I will," answered Effie, and held it fast until the last smiling face was gone, the surprise all over, and she safe in her own bed, too tired and happy for anything but sleep.

"Mamma, it *was* a beautiful surprise, and I thank you so much! I don't see how you ever did it; but I like it best of all the Christmases I ever had, and mean to make one every year. I had my splendid big present, and here is the dear little one to keep for love of poor Katy; so even that part of my wish came true."

And Effie fell asleep with a happy smile on her lips, her one humble gift still in her hand, and a new love for Christmas in her heart that never changed through a long life spent in doing good.

The Little Match-Girl

Hans Christian Andersen

IT WAS TERRIBLY COLD; IT SNOWED AND WAS ALREADY almost dark, and evening came on, the last evening of the year. In the cold and gloom a poor little girl, bare-headed and barefoot, was walking through the streets. When she left her own house she certainly had had slippers on, but of what use were they? They were very big slippers, and her mother had used them till then, so big were they. The little maid lost them as she slipped across the road, where two carriages were rattling by terribly fast. One slipper was not to be found again, and a boy had seized the other and run away with it. He thought he could use it very well as a cradle some day when he had children of his own. So now the little girl went with her little naked feet, which were quite red and blue with the cold. In an old apron she carried a number of matches, and a bundle of them in her hand. No one had bought anything of her all day, and no one had given her a farthing.

Shivering with cold and hunger, she crept along, a picture of misery, poor little girl! The snowflakes covered her long fair hair, which fell in pretty curls over her neck; but she did not think of that now. In all the windows lights were shining, and there was a glorious smell of roast goose, for it was New Year's Eve. Yes, she thought of that!

In a corner formed by two houses, one of which projected beyond the other, she sat down, cowering. She had drawn up her little feet, but she was still colder, and she did not dare to go home, for she had sold no matches and did not bring a farthing of money. From her father she would certainly receive a beating; and, besides, it was cold at home, for they had nothing over them but a roof through which the wind whistled, though the largest rents had been stopped with straw and rags.

Her little hands were almost benumbed with the cold. Ah, a match might do her good, if she could only draw one from the bundle and rub it against the wall and warm her hands at it. She drew one out. R-r-atch! how it sputtered and burned! It was a warm, bright flame, like a little candle, when she held her hands over it; it was a wonderful little light! It really seemed to the little girl as if she sat before a great polished stove with bright brass feet and a brass cover. How the fire burned! How comfortable it was! But the little flame went out, the stove vanished, and she had only the remains of the burnt match in her hand.

A second was rubbed against the wall. It burned up, and when the light fell upon the wall it became transparent like a thin veil, and she could see through it into the room. On the table a snow-white cloth was spread; upon it stood a shining dinner service; the roast goose smoked gloriously, stuffed with apples and dried plums. And, what was still more splendid to behold, the goose hopped down from the dish and waddled along the floor, with a knife and fork in its breast, to the little girl. Then the match went out and only the thick, damp, cold wall was before her. She lighted another match. Then she was sitting under a beautiful Christmas tree; it was greater and more ornamented than the one she had seen through the glass door at the rich merchant's. Thousands of candles burned upon the green branches, and colored pictures like those in the print shops looked down upon them. The little girl stretched forth her hand toward them; then the match went out. The Christmas lights mounted higher. She saw them now as stars in the sky; one of them fell down, forming a long line of fire.

"Now someone is dying," thought the little girl, for her old grandmother, the only person who had loved her, and who was now dead, had told her that when a star fell down a soul mounted up to God.

She rubbed another match against the wall; it became bright again, and in the brightness the old grandmother stood clear and shining, mild and lovely.

"Grandmother!" cried the child. "Oh, take me with you! I know you will go when the match is burned out. You will vanish like the warm fire, the warm food, and the great, glorious Christmas tree!"

And she hastily rubbed the whole bundle of matches, for she wished to hold her grandmother fast. And the matches burned with such a glow that it became brighter than in the middle of the day; grandmother had never been so large or so beautiful. She took the little girl in her arms, and both flew in brightness and joy above the earth, very, very high, and up there was neither cold, nor hunger, nor care — they were with God.

But in the corner, leaning against the wall, sat the poor girl with red cheeks and smiling mouth, frozen to death on the last evening of the old year. The New Year's sun rose upon a little corpse! The child sat there, stiff and cold, with the matches, of which one bundle was burned. "She wanted to warm herself," the people said. No one imagined what a beautiful thing she had seen and in what glory she had gone in with her grandmother to the New Year's Day.

APPLE Classics

Exciting adventures that kids everywhere have loved for a long time...so will you!

☐ MA43880-8	**Aesop's Fables** Ann McGovern	$2.75
☐ MA42035-6	**Alice in Wonderland** Lewis Carroll	$2.50
☐ MA42243-X	**Anne of Green Gables** L.M. Montgomery	$2.95
☐ MA43053-X	**Around the World in Eighty Days** Jules Verne	$2.95
☐ MA42118-2	**The Birds' Christmas Carol** Kate Douglas Wiggin	$2.50
☐ MA44724-8	**Captains Courageous** Rudyard Kipling	$2.95
☐ MA43527-2	**A Christmas Carol** Charles Dickens	$2.75
☐ MA42146-8	**Five Children and It** E. Nesbit	$2.95
☐ MA41295-7	**Hans Brinker or The Silver Skates** Mary Mapes Dodge	$2.95
☐ MA42046-1	**Heidi** Johanna Spyri	$2.95
☐ MA44016-0	**The Invisible Man** H.G. Wells	$2.95
☐ MA40719-8	**A Little Princess** Frances Hodgson Burnett	$2.95
☐ MA41279-5	**Little Men** Louisa May Alcott	$2.95
☐ MA43797-6	**Little Women** Louisa May Alcott	$2.95
☐ MA44769-6	**Pollyanna** Eleanor H. Porter	$2.95
☐ MA43283-4	**The Prince and the Pauper** Mark Twain	$2.75
☐ MA44025-X	**The Princess and the Goblin** George MacDonald	$2.95
☐ MA41343-0	**Rebecca of Sunnybrook Farm** Kate Douglas Wiggin	$2.95
☐ MA43285-0	**Robinson Crusoe** Daniel Defoe	$2.95
☐ MA43346-6	**The Secret Garden** Frances Hodgson Burnett	$2.95
☐ MA44014-4	**The Swiss Family Robinson** Johann Wyss	$3.25
☐ MA44774-2	**The Wind in the Willows** Kenneth Grahame	$2.95
☐ MA44089-6	**The Wizard of Oz** L. Frank Baum	$2.95

Available wherever you buy books, or use this order form.

Scholastic Inc., P.O. Box 7502, 2931 East McCarty Street, Jefferson City, MO 65102

Please send me the books I have checked above. I am enclosing $ _____ (please add $2.00 to cover shipping and handling). Send check or money order — no cash or C.O.D.s please.

Name_____

Address _____

City_____ State/Zip _____

Please allow four to six weeks for delivery. Available in the U.S. only. Sorry, mail orders are not available to residents of Canada. Prices subject to change.

AC1190

Society

Ske dies